MW01596440

Twice as Nice

by Knit Picks

Copyright © 2018 Knit Picks

All rights reserved. This book or any portion thereof
may not be reproduced or used in any manner
whatsoever without the express written permission
of the publisher except for the use of brief
quotations in a book review.

Photography by Amy Setter

Printed in the United States of America

First Printing, 2018

ISBN 978-1-62767-211-5

Versa Press, Inc

800-447-7829

www.versapress.com

CONTENTS

The holidays are such a personal time of the year. With childhood traditions and individual rituals, everyone has their own unique way of celebrating. There's no one right way to enjoy this joyful time whether you enjoy raucous gatherings flowing with merriment or cozy evenings in front of a yule log fire with your closest friends.

In that spirit, this collection gives you twice the choice, with options for every pattern; modern or traditional; naughty or nice; easy or hard. Make your holiday knitting truly *yours*, whether your personal Yuletide style includes lights and tinsel hanging from every surface or you prefer simpler expressions of the holidays.

Your style. Your traditions.

Your holidays.

BLIZZARD BAG HOLIDAY GIFT TOTES

by Sherrie Kibler

FINISHED MEASUREMENTS

7" wide x 9" high x 4" deep; 15" long handles.

YARN

Fair Isle Snowflake Tote:

Knit Picks Wool of the Andes Worsted (100% Peruvian Highland Wool; 110 yards/50g): MC Delft Heather 25649, 2 balls; C2 White 24065, 1 ball.

Mosaic Snowman Tote:

Knit Picks Wool of the Andes Worsted (100% Peruvian Highland Wool; 110 yards/50g): MC Delft Heather 25649, 1 ball; C1 Lake Ice Heather 23898, 1 ball; C2 White 24065, 2 balls.

NEEDLES

US 7 (4.5mm) circular needles, or size to obtain gauge.

NOTIONS

Yarn Needle
Stitch Marker
Size I-9 (5.5mm) Crochet Hook
Poster Board: 20.5x15.5" per bag
1.5", 2", 2.5" Pom Pom Maker

Notes:

Both totes are worked upward in the round from a flat, rectangular seed stitch base with rounded corners. The facing that cleanly folds down to the inside of the tote provides additional support for the crocheted carrying ties. A removable liner is cut from poster board and tied in place at the tote's corners.

When working a chart in the rnd, read each row from right to left as a RS row, knitting all sts unless charted otherwise.

Seed Stitch (worked flat or in the rnd over an even number of sts)
Row/Rnd 1: *P1, K1; rep from * to end.
Row/Rnd 2: *K1, P1; rep from * end.
Rep Rows/Rnds 1 and 2 for pattern.

PU & K TBL: Hold the yarn to the back, insert your RH needle from front to back through the opening between 2 picked up edge sts of the last rnd; wrap your yarn around the RH needle and pull the loop to the front. Place the loop onto the LH needle and K TBL. 1 st inc.

DIRECTIONS

Fair Isle Snowflake Tote
Tote Base (worked flat)
With MC, CO 14 sts.
Row 1: KFB, (K1, P1) 6 times, KFB. 16 sts.
Row 2: KFB, (K1, P1) 7 times, KFB. 18 sts.
Work 49 rows of Seed Stitch pattern.
Next Row: K2tog, (K1, P1) 7 times, K2tog. 16 sts.
Next Row: K2tog, (K1, P1) 6 times, K2tog. 14 sts.

Sides of Tote (worked in the rnd)
Leave the 14 sts on needle then use MC to PU 66 additional sts as follows: PU 1 st at each corner, PU 24 sts along each of the two long sides, and PU 14 sts on the opposite short side of the base. 80 sts. PM for start of rnd and prepare to work in the rnd.

Next Rnd: K15, (K2, PU & K TBL) 12 times, K16, (K2, PU & K TBL) 12 times, K1. 104 sts.
Work the Fair Isle Chart, rep the chart twice across each rnd. Break C2, work remainder in MC.

Facing
Next Rnd: P all sts.
Next Rnd: K all sts.
Next Rnd: K2tog 3 times, K4, K2tog 8 times, K16, K2tog 8 times, K4, K2tog 8 times, K16, K2tog 5 times. 72 sts.
Work in St st (K all rnds) for 1.75" then work 3 rnds of Seed Stitch. BO loosely. Weave in ends.

Liner
Cut a piece of poster board into a 20.5" x 15.5" rectangle. Refer to the Liner Diagram as you cut the liner shape along

the solid lines and fold along the dashed lines. Fold to form an open-ended rectangular shape; tape the corner fold and bottom in a few places. Use a sharp needle to pierce the liner to locate holes for the carrying ties about 1.5" from the top and side of the liner as indicated on the diagram.

Carrying Ties
Use 2 strands of C2 or desired color and the crochet hook to chain two ties, each 21" in length. Leave 6" yarn lengths at each end.

Blocking
To use the assembled liner as a blocking form, place a plastic bag over the liner, then place the finished knitted tote over the protected liner. Lightly steam block the tote in place on the form.

Tote Assembly
Place the blocked tote over the liner, centering the snowflake motif across the length of the tote. Fold down the facing, and temporarily tape the facing in place on the inside. Thread 12" lengths of MC yarn at each of the facing's four corners to act as facing anchor ties. With one end of the first anchor tie threaded through a sharp needle, use the needle to pierce the liner at the corner and discreetly pull the anchor tie to the outside of the tote and back to the inside where it can be tied in a bow to its opposite end. Rep for the remaining corners.

Thread the needle through the double yarn strands at one end of a Carrying Tie. Carefully weave the needle with attached Carrying Tie from the outside of the tote, through the pre-located holes of the liner, and through the facing to the inside. NOTE: Use care to run the needle and strands between sts and rows so you don't pierce/split the knitted sts with the needle tip. Rep for the other end of the carrying tie, then double-knot both carrying tie ends on the inside of the tote. Work ends into knots. Rep for the second carrying tie on the opposite side of the tote.

Mosaic Snowman Tote
Tote Base (worked flat)
Work the same as the Fair Isle Snowflake Tote.

Sides of Tote (worked in the rnd)
PU sts along the sides and corners as outlined in the Fair Isle Snowflake Tote. 80 sts. PM for start of rnd and to prepare to work in the rnd.
Next Rnd: K15, (K6, PU & K TBL) 4 times, K16, (K6, M1L) 4 times, K1. 88 sts.
Work the Mosaic Chart, rep the chart 44 times across each rnd. Break MC and C1, work remainder in C2.

Facing
Next Rnd: P all sts.
Next Rnd: K all sts.

Next Rnd: K2tog 3 times, K4, K2tog 6 times, K16, K2tog 6 times, K4, K2tog 6 times, K16, K2tog 3 times. 64 sts.
Work in St st (K all rnds) for 1.75", then work 3 rnds of Seed Stitch. BO loosely. Weave in ends.

Snowman Base
The pom-pom snowman is attached to a rectangular Seed Stitch Snowman Base piece. This allows the completed snowman assembly to be easily attached to the side of the tote.

With C2, CO 4 sts. Work Seed Stitch for 3". BO loosely.

Snowman
Make 3 C2 pom-poms of descending diameters: 2.5", 2", and 1.5". Leave long ends for assembly. If desired, you can start with 3 2.5" pom-poms and trim to the smaller sizes.

Snowman Scarf (worked flat)
With MC, CO 4 sts.
Rows 1-2: Work in St st (K on RS, P on WS).
Row 3 (RS): *K1 in C2, K1 in MC; rep from * to end of row.
Row 4 (WS): *P1 in C2, P1 in MC; rep from * to end of row.
Break C2. Work 7" of St st in MC, ending on a WS row.
Rep Rows 3-4. Break C2.
Next 2 Rows: Using MC, work in St st MC.
BO loosely. Use the crochet hook to attach C2 fringe to ends of Scarf.

Snowman Hat
The snowman's hat is worked flat in MC and seamed upon completion. CO 20 sts.
Rows 1-6: Work in St st.
Row 7: *K3, K2tog; rep from * to end. 16 sts.
Row 8: P all sts.
Row 9: *K2, K2tog; rep from * to end. 12 sts.
Row 10: P all sts.
Row 11: *K1, K2tog; rep from * to end. 8 sts.
Cut yarn, leaving a 10" tail. Pull tail through remaining 8 sts, then use tail to seam hat.

Liner, Carrying Ties, Blocking
Create the same as the Fair Isle Snowflake Tote.

Snowman Assembly
Place the three pom-poms close together on the Snowman Base to form the snowman. Use the pom-pom ends to attach the pom-poms to the Snowman Base. Roll the brim of the hat then position the hat on the snowman's head and stitch it to the Snowman Base; stitch the midpoint of the scarf to the Snowman Base under the smallest pom-pom, and tie the scarf around the snowman's neck.

Tote Assembly
Attach the Snowman Assembly to the tote about 1" from the tote bottom and centered across the length of the tote. Complete the tote assembly the same as the Fair Isle tote.

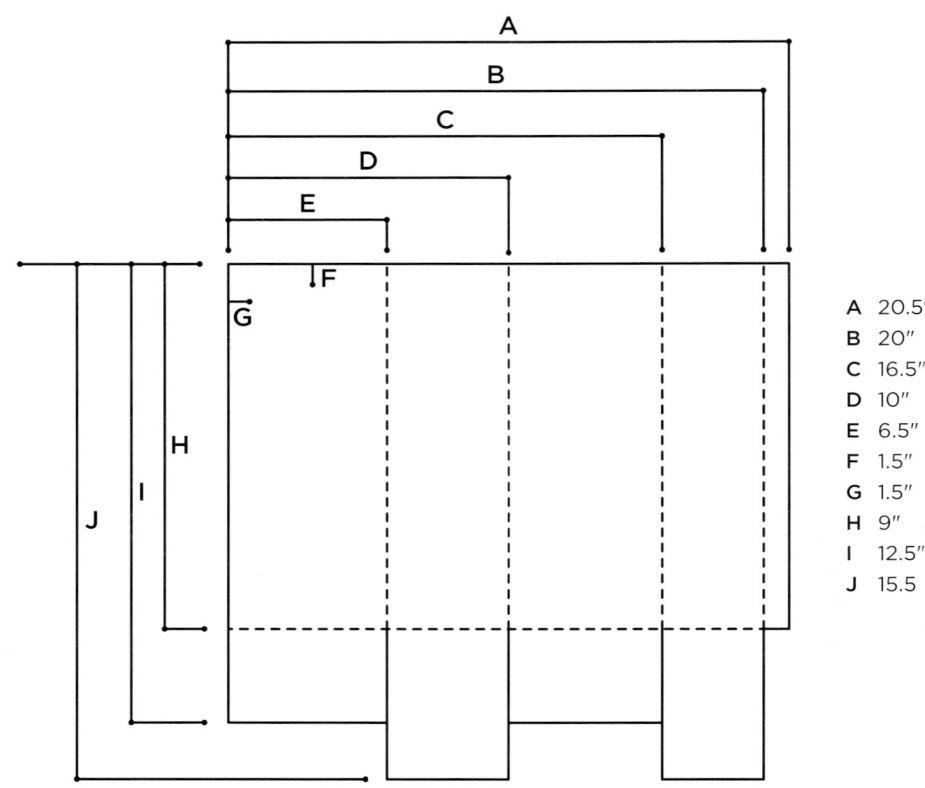

A 20.5″
B 20″
C 16.5″
D 10″
E 6.5″
F 1.5″
G 1.5″
H 9″
I 12.5″
J 15.5

Liner cut/assembled size: 6.5 x 3.5 x 9″
To make final tote measurements: 7 x 4 x 9″
Note: Diagram is not to scale.

Fair Isle Chart

Legend

- ☐ **K** — Knit stitch
- ⦿ **P** — Purl stitch
- ⩗ **Slip Stitch (sl)** — Slip stitch as if to purl with yarn in back.
- ⩔ **Slip WYIF** — Slip stitch as if to purl with yarn in front.
- ▭ **Pattern Repeat**
- ▪ **MC**
- ▨ **C1**
- ☐ **C2**

Mosaic Chart

Scarf Chart

	4	3	2	1
2		■	■	■
	■		■		1

CABINS AND POINSETTIAS SACHETS

by Simone Kereit

FINISHED MEASUREMENTS

5" wide x 5.5" high.

YARN

Cabins:

Knit Picks Palette

(100% Peruvian Highland Wool; 231 yards/50g): MC Clarity 25548, C1 Grizzly Heather 25532, C2 Forest Heather 24584; 1 ball each.

Poinsettias:

Knit Picks Palette

(100% Peruvian Highland Wool; 231 yards/50g): MC Clarity 25548, C1 Hollyberry 25539, C2 Turmeric 24251; 1 ball each.

NEEDLES

US 2 (2.75mm) DPNs or one 32" or longer circular needle for Magic Loop technique, or size to obtain gauge. Circular needles for Judy's Magic Cast On.

NOTIONS

Yarn Needle
Stitch Markers
Dried Lavender, Dried Rose Petals, or Potpourri

GAUGE

32 sts and 36 rounds = 4" in stranded St st in the round, blocked.

Notes:

The Cabins and Poinsettia Sachets are a sweet little gift for anyone on your list. Who doesn't like their laundry drawer to have a nice natural scent? And if you are newer to fair isle and stranded colorwork, they are a great way to get your feet wet without too much commitment!

I like to make thoughtful gifts and often find I have people with different tastes on my list and one pattern is just not going to fit all. So, if like me, you have a variety of folks on your list, this little gift set gives you two options. Choose from a classic holiday design featuring iconic poinsettias or go for a modern woodsy version with cabins in the woods!

When knitting stranded colorwork designs, on rounds that use two colors, carry both yarns on the wrong side of your work, making sure not to pull too tight but leaving floats loose. Anytime your floats are longer than 4 stitches, catch the float in the back by twisting the two yarns around each other.

Charts are worked in the rnd; read each row from right to left as a RS row.

Judy's Magic CO: Using circular needles, make a slip knot, leaving a long enough tail to CO half the sts. Holding needles parallel, place slip knot on top needle. Hold yarn similar to working a Long Tail CO, but with tail end over your index finger and working end over your thumb. Using a figure 8 motion, bring tail end yarn from your index finger all the way down and counter clockwise around bottom needle, then to the back in between the two needles; then bring working yarn from your thumb around the back to the top of the top needle and clockwise over that needle, through between the two needles to the back.

Counting the slip knot as st 1, CO the required number of sts, half on each needle. Turn clockwise until both needle tips point to the right, then gently pull bottom needle until sts rest on cord and you can comfortably start knitting the sts on top needle. Using preferred needles (DPNs or the circular needles you used for CO), knit sts on top needle, then working in the rnd, knit sts on bottom needle TBL.

There is also a Knit Picks video tutorial for a slightly different way here:
https://tutorials.knitpicks.com/judys-magic-cast-on/

DIRECTIONS
With MC and Judy's Magic CO, CO 80 sts. PM for beginning of rnd, K 40 sts, then K the next 40 sts TBL.

With MC, K 2 rounds even, then work Rnds 1-47 of Poinsettia or Cabins chart, repeating chart 4 times per rnd and changing colors as indicated.
BO in MC.

Finishing
Weave in ends, wash and block.

When completely dry, fill with dried lavender, dried rose petals from your garden or potpourri. The easiest way to do this is to use the foot of tights/nylons or a thin sock. Fill this with lavender, draw top of sock over itself, then insert the closed sock into the sachet. With yarn in the same color as the BO rnd, whip stitch top of sachet closed. Attach optional mini tassels to each corner of the sachet.

Mini Tassels (make 4, optional)
Using a piece of sturdy cardboard approximately 2" long as a template, wrap yarn (Grizzly Heather for Cabins, Hollyberry for Poinsettia) around 10 to 14 times, starting and ending at the bottom edge. Hold yarn double, insert a piece of the same yarn through the top center of the wraps and tie snuggly. Slip yarn loops off the template.

Cut a length of yarn about 6" long and fold in half. Tightly wrap the doubled yarn around the tassel about 0.5" from the tied off top. Knot securely and pull ends through center of the tassels and to the bottom using a darning needle. Cut bottom ends of yarn open, trim even if necessary and sew tassel to the corners of the sachet.

A little steam from a steam iron held just above the tassels will help fluff them up nicely!

Cabins Chart

Legend

K
Knit stitch

MC

Cabins

C1

C2

Poinsettias

C1

C2

Poinsettias Chart

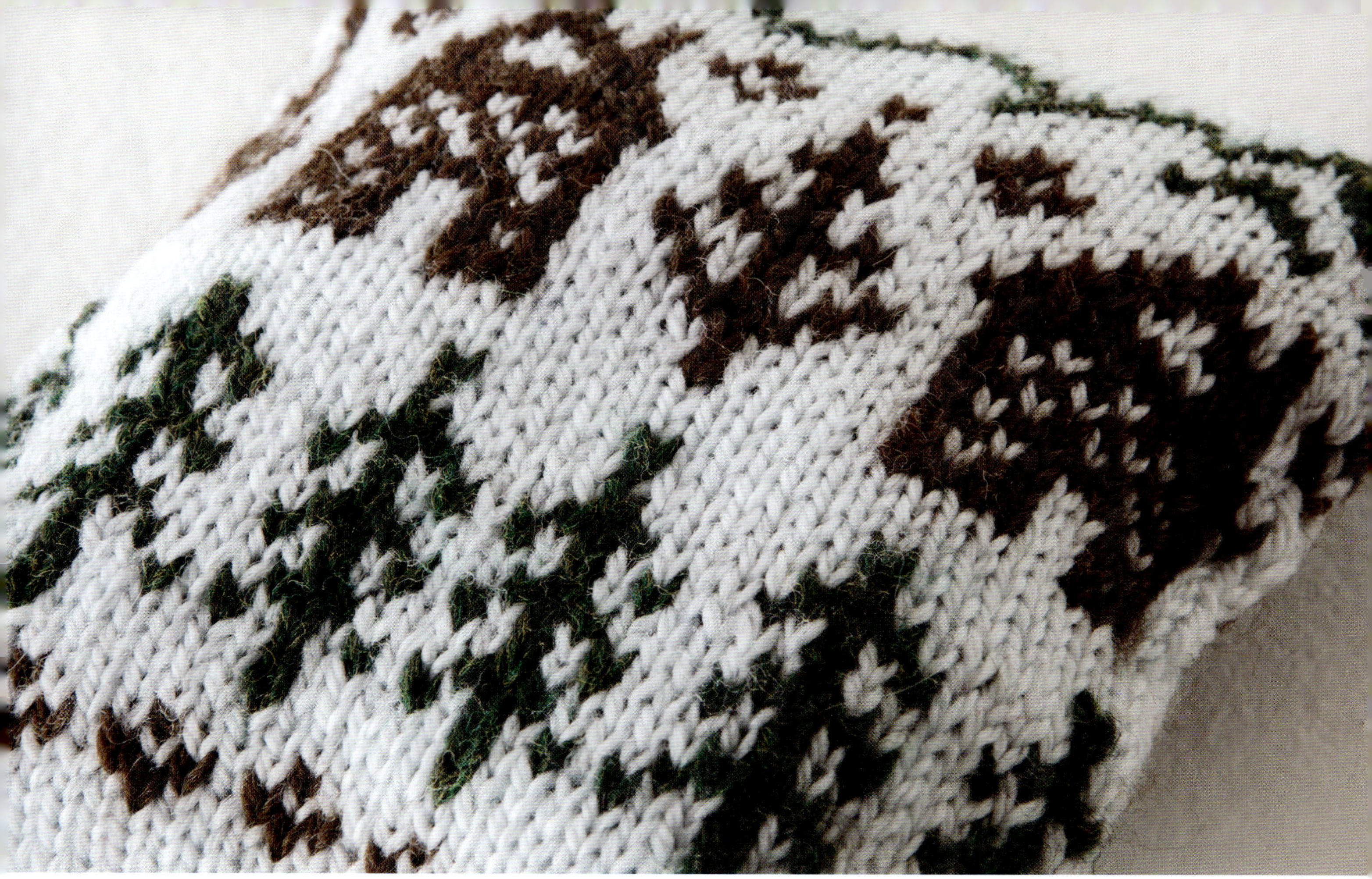

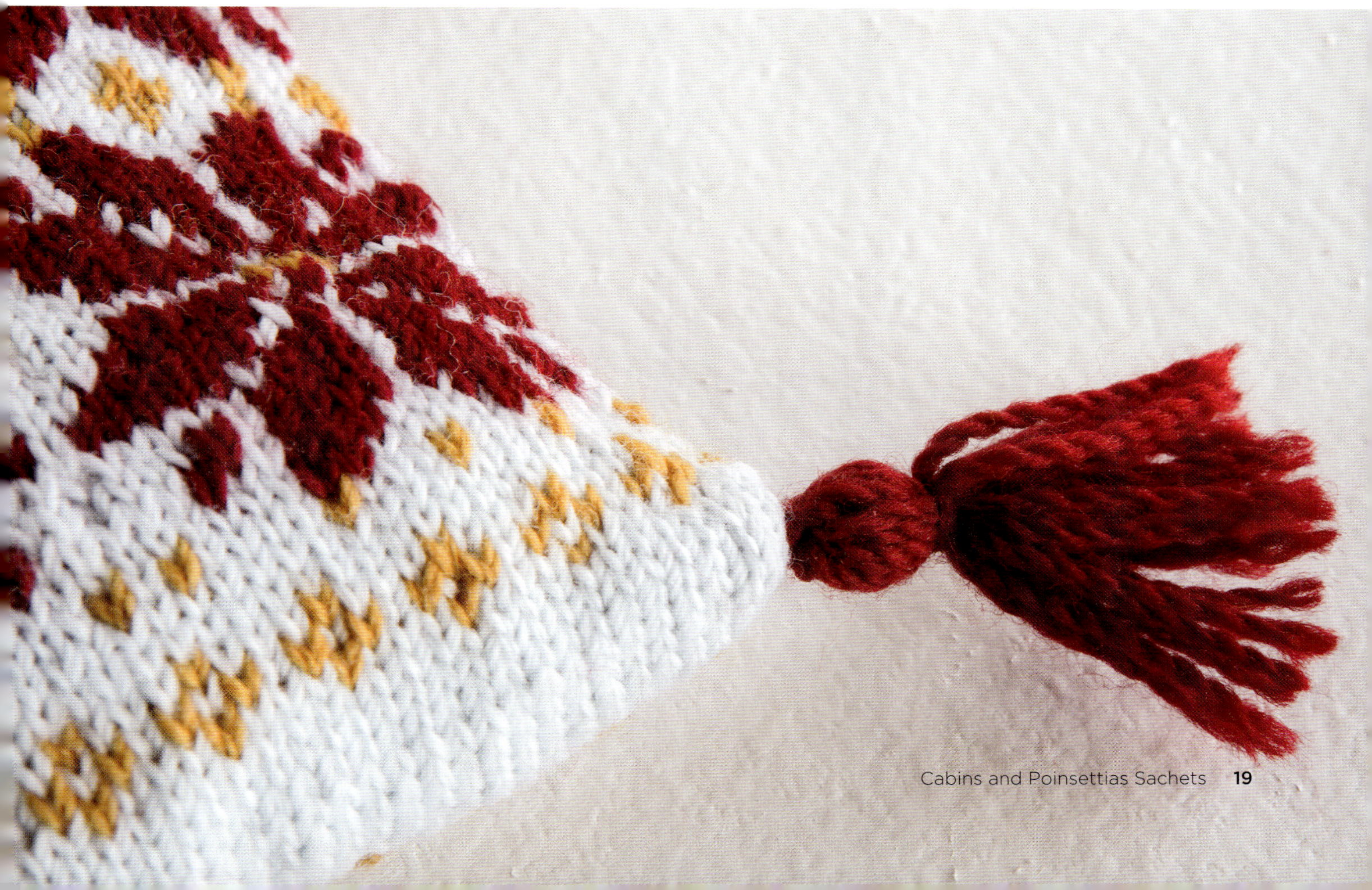

COAL VS. SNOWPEOPLE

by Knit Picks Design Team

FINISHED MEASUREMENTS

Coal: 1.75" high x 2" wide.
Snowpeople: Slim: 5" tall, including hat;
Rosy: 3" tall; Lumpy: 3.5" tall,
including hat.

YARN

Knit Picks Stroll Glimmer
(70% Fine Superwash Merino Wool, 25%
Nylon, 5% Stellina): C1 Midnight Heather
27541, C2 White 25493, C3 Scarlett
27543, C4 Peacock 25485, C5 Regal
27542, C6 Frost 25495; 1 ball each

NEEDLES

US 0 (2mm) DPNs or two 24" circular
needles for two circulars technique,
or one 32" or longer circular needle
for Magic Loop technique, or size to
obtain gauge.

NOTIONS

Yarn Needle
Fiberfill
(8) 6mm Safety Eyes
(3) 10mm buttons
Stitch Markers
Small Crochet Hook (optional)

GAUGE

36 sts and 48 rows = 4" in St st in the
round (exact gauge is not important, but
the fabric should be tight enough so the
fiberfill does not show though the sts).

Notes:

Naughty or nice? You'll be able to make everyone on your list one of these cute little toys. For the "naughty" folks, Grumpy the Lump of Coal is much cuter than the real thing and will bring a smile to your giftee's face. For the "nice" folks, choose from 3 different snow people – or make all three for a cute decoration.

All 4 toys are knit in the round, and you can make several from one skein of yarn. Only small amounts of the contrast colors are needed for the snow people's accessories. Safety eyes are used in this pattern, but you can also use scrap yarn to embroider the faces.

DIRECTIONS

Grumpy, the Lump of Coal

With C1, CO 6 sts, join to knit in the rnd being careful not to twist sts, and knit one rnd. PM to mark beginning of rnd.

Rnd 2: *K1, M1* to end. 12 sts.

Rnd 3: K.

Rnd 4: Rep Rnd 2. 24 sts.

Rnd 5: *K4, M1* to end. 30 sts.

Rnd 6: *K7, M1, K8, M1* twice. 34 sts.

Rnd 7: *K8, M1, K9, M1* twice. 38 sts.

Rnd 8: *K9, M1, K10, M1* twice. 42 sts.

Rnd 9: *K21, M1* twice. 44 sts.

Rnd 10: K11, M1, K22, M1, K11. 46 sts.

Rnd 11: *K23, M1* twice. 48 sts.

Rnd 12: K12, M1, K24, M1, K12. 50 sts.

Rnd 13: K.

Rnd 14: *K23, K2tog* twice. 48 sts.

Rnd 15: K.

Rnd 16: K11, K2tog, K22, K2tog, K11. 46 sts.

Rnd 17: K.

Rnd 18: *K21, K2tog* twice. 44 sts.

Rnd 19: K10, K2tog, K20, K2tog, K10. 42 sts.

Rnd 20: *K5, K2tog* to end. 36 sts.

Rnd 21: *K4, K2tog* to end. 30 sts.

Rnd 22: *K3, K2tog* to end. 24 sts.

Rnd 23: K.

Rnd 24: *K10, K2tog* twice. 22 sts.

Rnd 25: *K9, K2tog* twice. 20 sts.

Rnd 26: K.

Stuff the lower portion of the coal lightly at this point.

Rnd 27: *K8, K2tog* twice. 18 sts.

Rnd 28: K.

Rnd 29: *K7, K2tog* twice. 16 sts.

Rnd 30: *K2, K2tog* to end. 12 sts.

Finish stuffing the coal. Add safety eyes at approximately Rnd 23.

Rnd 31: *K1, K2tog* to end. 8 sts.

Cut yarn and draw tail through live sts, pulling tightly to draw the opening closed.

Finishing

Weave in ends.

Slim

Slim is a tall gentleman snowman with three distinct sections.

Lower Body Section

With C2, CO 6 sts, join to knit in the rnd being careful not to twist sts, and knit one rnd. PM to mark beginning of rnd.

Rnd 2: *K1, M1* to end. 12 sts.
Rnd 3: K.
Rnd 4: *K1, M1* to end. 24 sts.
Rnd 5: *K4, M1* to end. 30 sts.
Rnd 6: *K7, M1, K8, M1* twice. 34 sts.
Rnd 7: *K8, M1, K9, M1* twice. 38 sts.
Rnd 8: *K9, M1, K10, M1* twice. 42 sts.
Rnd 9: *K21, M1* twice. 44 sts.
Rnd 10: K11, M1, K22, M1, K11. 46 sts.
Rnd 11: *K23, M1* twice. 48 sts.
Rnd 12: K12, M1, K24, M1, K12. 50 sts.
Rnds 13-16: K.
Rnd 17: *K23, K2tog* twice. 48 sts.
Rnd 18: K.
Rnd 19: K11, K2tog, K22, K2tog, K11. 46 sts.
Rnd 20: K.
Rnd 21: *K21, K2tog* twice. 44 sts.
Rnd 22: K10, K2tog, K20, K2tog, K10. 42 sts.
Rnd 23: *K5, K2tog* to end. 36 sts.

Upper Body Section

Rnd 1: *K4, K2tog* to end. 30 sts.
Rnd 2: *K15, M1* twice. 32 sts.
Rnd 3: *K8, M1* to end. 36 sts.
Rnd 4: *K18, M1* twice. 38 sts.
Rnd 5: K9, M1, K20, M1, K to end. 40 sts.
Rnd 6: K.
Rnd 7: *K20, M1* twice. 42 sts.
Rnds 8-10: K.
Rnd 11: *K19, K2tog* twice. 40 sts.
Rnd 12: K9, K2tog, K18, K2tog, K to end. 38 sts.
Rnd 13: *K17, K2tog* twice. 36 sts.
Rnd 14: *K7, K2tog* to end. 32 sts.
Rnd 15: *K6, K2tog* to end. 28 sts.
Rnd 16: *K5, K2tog* to end. 24 sts.

Head Section

Rnd 1: K.
Rnd 2: *K12, M1* twice. 26 sts.
Rnd 3: K6, M1, K14, M1, K6. 28 sts.
Rnd 4: *K14, M1* twice. 30 sts.
Rnd 5: K7, M1, K16, M1, K7. 32 sts.
Rnd 6: *K16, M1* twice. 34 sts.
Rnds 7-8: K.

Stuff body section.
Rnd 9: K7, K2tog, K16, K2tog, K7. 32 sts.
Rnd 10: *K14, K2tog* twice. 30 sts.

Rnd 11: *K6, K2tog, K5, K2tog* twice. 26 sts.
Rnd 12: *K2, K2tog, K3, K2tog* twice, K2, K2tog, K2, K2tog. 20 sts.
Rnd 13: *K1, K2tog* 5 times, K2, K2tog, K1. 14 sts.
Stuff head. Add safety eyes at approximately Rnd 11.
Rnd 14: *K2tog* to end. 7 sts.
Draw yarn tail through remaining sts and pull snug, securing end.

Top Hat

With C1, CO 9 sts, join to knit in the rnd being careful not to twist sts, and knit one rnd. PM to mark beginning of rnd.

Rnd 2: KFB across. 18 sts.
Rnds 3-5: K.
Rnd 6: P.
Rnds 7-12: Knit.
Rnd 13: *K4, K2tog* 3 times. 15 sts.
Rnd 14-19: K.
Rnd 20: KFB across. 30 sts.
Rnd 21: K.
BO in P.

Long Skinny Scarf

CO 3 sts with C3, Work I-cord for approximately 18" or to reach length desired, BO. Add small pieces of yarn as fringe, if desired.

Finishing

Weave in any remaining ends. Sew hat to top of Slim's head. Wrap scarf around Slim's neck and secure. With C1, add a nose. Attach buttons to upper body section.

Rosy

Rosy is a petite and curvaceous snow-woman with a generous body section.

Lower Body Section

With C2, CO 6 sts, join to knit in the rnd being careful not to twist sts, and knit one rnd. PM to mark beginning of rnd.

Rnd 2: *K1, M1* to end. 12 sts.
Rnd 3: K.
Rnd 4: *K1, M1* to end. 24 sts.
Rnd 5: *K4, M1* to end. 30 sts.
Rnd 6: *K7, M1, K8, M1* twice. 34 sts.
Rnd 7: *K8, M1, K9, M1* twice. 38 sts.
Rnd 8: *K9, M1, K10, M1* twice. 42 sts.
Rnd 9: *K21, M1* twice. 44 sts.
Rnd 10: K11, M1, K22, M1, K11. 46 sts.
Rnd 11: *K23, M1* twice. 48 sts.
Rnd 12: K12, M1, K24, M1, K12. 50 sts.
Rnds 13-18: K.
Rnd 19: *K23, K2tog* twice. 48 sts.
Rnd 20: K.
Rnd 21: K11, K2tog, K22, K2tog, K11. 46 sts.

Rnd 22: K.
Rnd 23: *K21, K2tog* twice. 44 sts.
Rnd 24: K10, K2tog, K20, K2tog, K10. 42 sts.
Rnd 25: *K5, K2tog* to end. 36 sts.
Rnd 26: *K4, K2tog* to end. 30 sts.
Rnd 27: *K3, K2tog* to end. 24 sts.

Head Section
Rnd 1: K.
Rnd 2: *K12, M1* twice. 26 sts.
Rnd 3: K6, M1, K14, M1, K6. 28 sts.
Rnd 4: *K14, M1* twice. 30 sts.
Rnd 5: K7, M1, K16, M1, K7. 32 sts.
Rnd 6: *K16, M1* twice. 34 sts.
Rnds 7-8: K.
Stuff body section.
Rnd 9: K7, K2tog, K16, K2tog, K7. 32 sts.
Rnd 10: *K14, K2tog* twice. 30 sts.
Rnd 11: *K6, K2tog, K5, K2tog* twice. 26 sts.
Rnd 12: *K2, K2tog, K3, K2tog* twice, K2, K2tog, K2, K2tog.
20 sts.
Rnd 13: *K1, K2tog* 5 times, K2, K2tog, K1. 14 sts.
Stuff head. Add safety eyes at approximately Rnd 9.
Rnd 14: *K2tog* to end. 7 sts.
Draw yarn tail through remaining sts and pull snug,
securing end.

Capelet
With C5, CO 32 sts, do not join.
Row 1 (WS): *K1, P1, rep to end.
Row 2 (RS): *P1, K1, rep to end
Row 3: P.

Row 4: K8, PM, M1L, K16, M1R, PM, K8. 34 sts.
Row 5: P.
Row 6: K to M, SM, M1L, K to M, M1R, SM, K to end. 2 sts inc.
Rep these last two rows 3 more times. 42 sts.
Next Row: P.
Rep Rows 1-2.
BO all sts. Weave in ends and block lightly. Crochet two 3"
chains or CO 2 sts and knit a small I-cord with C5 and attach
to collar for a tie closure, or use a decorative hook and clasp.

Ear Muffs
With C5 CO 2 sts and work 2" of I-cord. and BO, leaving
a generous yarn tail. Roll the I-cord into a circle and sew
together using yarn tails and crochet hook. Rep for second ear
muff. Attach the two ear muffs with a single crocheted chain.

Finishing
Weave in any remaining ends. Tie capelet around Rosy's
neck with a bow tie. Sew earmuffs to Rosy's head. With C1,
add a nose.

Lumpy
Lumpy is a spring snowman who may have once looked like
Slim, but now his sections are slowly melting together and
becoming less distinct.

Lower Body Section
With C2, CO 6 sts, join to knit in the rnd being careful not to
twist sts, and knit one rnd. PM to mark beginning of rnd.
Rnd 2: *K1, M1* to end. 12 sts.
Rnd 3: K.
Rnd 4: *K1, M1* to end. 24 sts.
Rnd 5: *K4, M1* to end. 30 sts.

Rnd 6: *K7, M1, K8, M1* twice. 34 sts.
Rnd 7: *K8, M1, K9, M1* twice. 38 sts.
Rnd 8: *K9, M1, K10, M1* twice. 42 sts.
Rnd 9: *K21, M1* twice. 44 sts.
Rnd 10: K11, M1, K22, M1, K11. 46 sts.
Rnd 11: *K23, M1* twice. 48 sts.
Rnd 12: K12, M1, K24, M1, K12. 50 sts.
Rnds 13-16: K.
Rnd 17: *K23, K2tog* twice. 48 sts.
Rnd 18: K.
Rnd 19: K11, K2tog, K22, K2tog, K11. 46 sts.
Rnd 20: K.
Rnd 21: *K21, K2tog* twice. 44 sts.
Rnd 22: K10, K2tog, K20, K2tog, K10. 42 sts.

Upper Body Section
Rnd 1: K.
Rnd 2: *K21, M1* twice. 44 sts.
Rnds 3-5: K.
Rnd 6: K10, K2tog, K20, K2tog, K10. 42 sts.
Rnd 7: *K19, K2tog* twice. 40 sts.
Rnd 8: *K4, K2tog, K5, K2tog* 3 times, K1. 34 sts.
Rnd 9: *K6, K2tog, K7, K2tog* twice. 30 sts.
Rnd 10: *K5, K2tog, K6, K2tog* twice. 26 sts.

Head Section
Rnd 1: *K13, M1* twice. 28 sts.
Rnd 2: K7, M1, K14, M1, K7. 30 sts.
Rnd 3: *K15, M1* twice. 32 sts.
Stuff body section.
Rnds 4-5: K.
Rnd 6: K7, K2tog, K14, K2tog, K7. 30 sts.
Rnd 7: *K13, K2tog* twice. 28 sts.

Rnd 8: K6, K2tog, K12, K2tog, K6. 26 sts.
Rnd 9: *K2, K2tog, K3, K2tog* twice, K2, K2tog, K2, K2tog. 20 sts.
Rnd 10: *K1, K2tog* 5 times, K2, K2tog, K1. 14 sts.
Stuff head. Add safety eyes at approximately Rnd 6.
Rnd 11: *K2tog* to end. 7 sts.
Draw yarn tail through remaining sts and pull snug, securing end.

Striped Scarf
Even though this is knit flat, it is much easier to use 2 DPNs, due to the small size. When attaching and cutting yarn, leave a 1" tail on each end for fringe.
Using C4, CO 56 sts.
Cut C4, join C6 and knit 1 row.
Cut C6, join C4 and knit 1 row.
Cut C4, join C6 and knit 1 row.
Cut C6, join C4 and BO.

Beanie
With C4, CO 32 sts, and join to knit in rnd, being careful not to twist sts. PM to mark beginning of rnd.
Rnds 1-2: *K1, P1, rep to end.
Change to C6.
Rnd 3-4: K.
Change to C4.
Rnd 5-6: K.
Rnd 7: K2tog across rnd. 16 sts.
Rnd 8: K.
Rnd 9: K2tog across rnd. 8 sts.
Cut yarn and draw yarn tail through.

Finishing
Weave in any remaining ends. Tie scarf around Lumpy's neck and secure. Attach beanie to top of Lumpy's head. With C1, add a nose.

DAY AND NIGHT CUP COZIES

by Violet LeBeaux

FINISHED MEASUREMENTS

8" Circumference x 3" high.

YARN

Knit Picks Stroll Sock Yarn
(75% Superwash Merino Wool, 25% Nylon; 231 yards/50g): MC White 26082, 1 ball; C1 Black 23701, 1 ball.

NEEDLES

US 3 (3mm) DPNs, or one 24" or longer circular needle for Magic Loop technique, or size to obtain gauge.

NOTIONS

5 x 1cm and 5 x 1.5cm buttons for Day Cozy design.
16 x 1cm buttons for Night Cozy design.
Yarn Needle
Scrap yarn for embroidered design
Stitch Markers

GAUGE

30 sts and 40 rows = 4" over St st in the round, blocked.

For pattern support, contact
violetlebeaux@gmail.com

Notes:

Day and Night is a simple set of matching holiday cup cozies that beginner knitters will love. The Day design features a light background with Christmas baubles hanging on strings while the Night design features a dark background with strings of Christmas lights weaving around the cup. Perfect for holiday gifts!

The cozy is a very easy knit with only stockinette and 1x1 ribbing; construction is bottom up, in the round. The strings are embroidered on after construction and buttons added to represent the baubles and lights. The simple construction makes them ideal travel projects for last-minute gifting.

DIRECTIONS

Cup Cozy

Using MC for Day design or C1 for Night design, loosely CO 60 sts, and join to work in the round.

Ribbing
Rnds 1-6: (K1, P1) to end.

Stockinette
Rnd 1: K to end.
Complete another 19 rnds in St st OR continue until work measures approximately 2" from beginning of section.

Ribbing
Rnds 1-6: (K1, P1) to end.
BO all sts.

Finishing

Weave in ends, wash and block to diagram.
Day Cup Cozy: Using C1, stitch the embroidered sections on to the cup cozy using Day Cup Cozy chart as a reference.
Night Cup Cozy: Using MC, stitch the embroidered sections on to the cup cozy using Night Cup Cozy chart as a reference.
Sew the buttons on as indicated in the chart and weave in any additional ends.

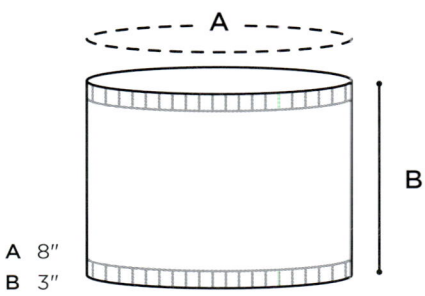

A 8"
B 3"

Day Coffee Cup Cozy Chart

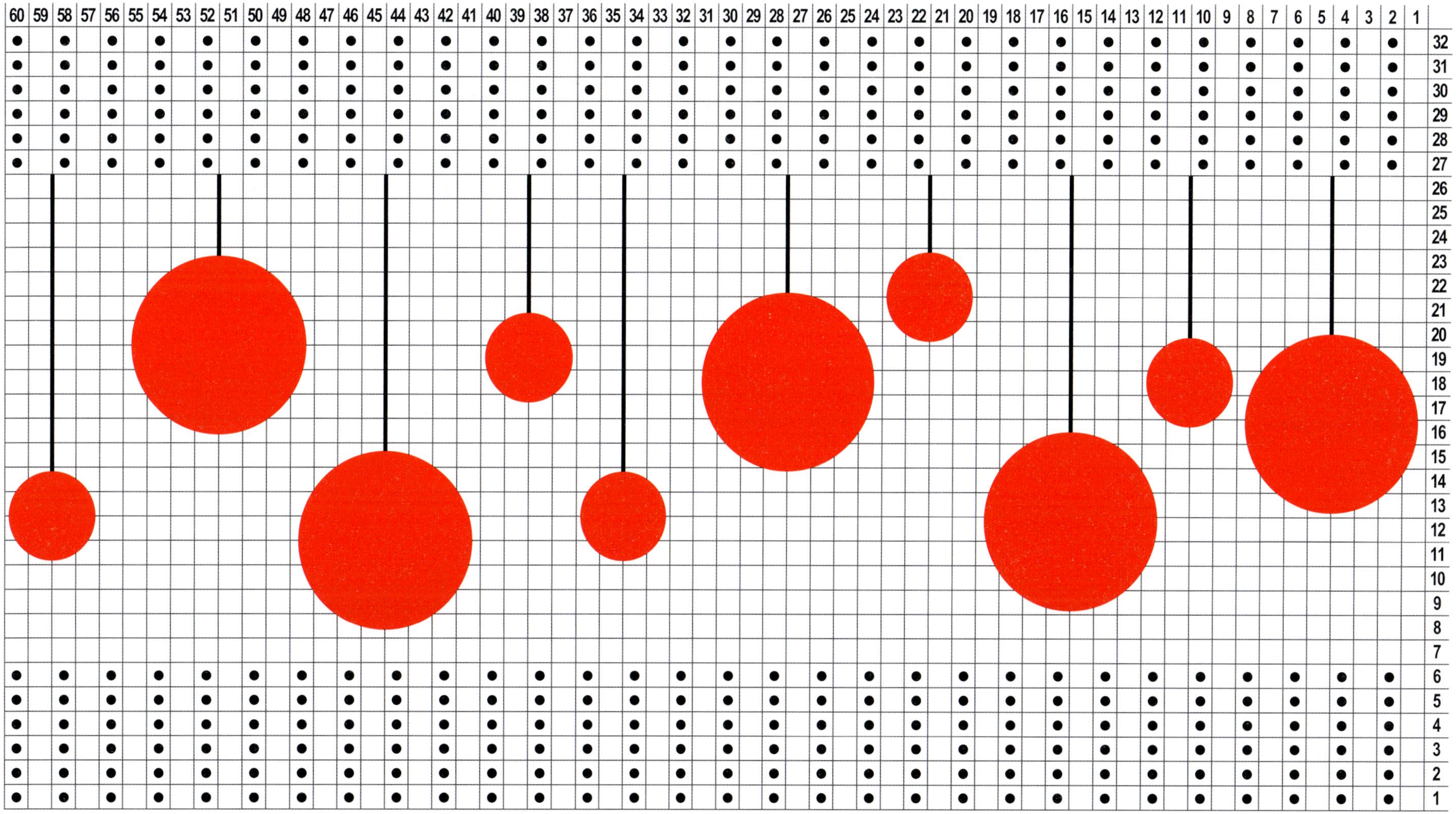

Legend

- K — Knit stitch
- P — Purl stitch
- Embroider
- Button

Night Coffee Cup Cozy Chart

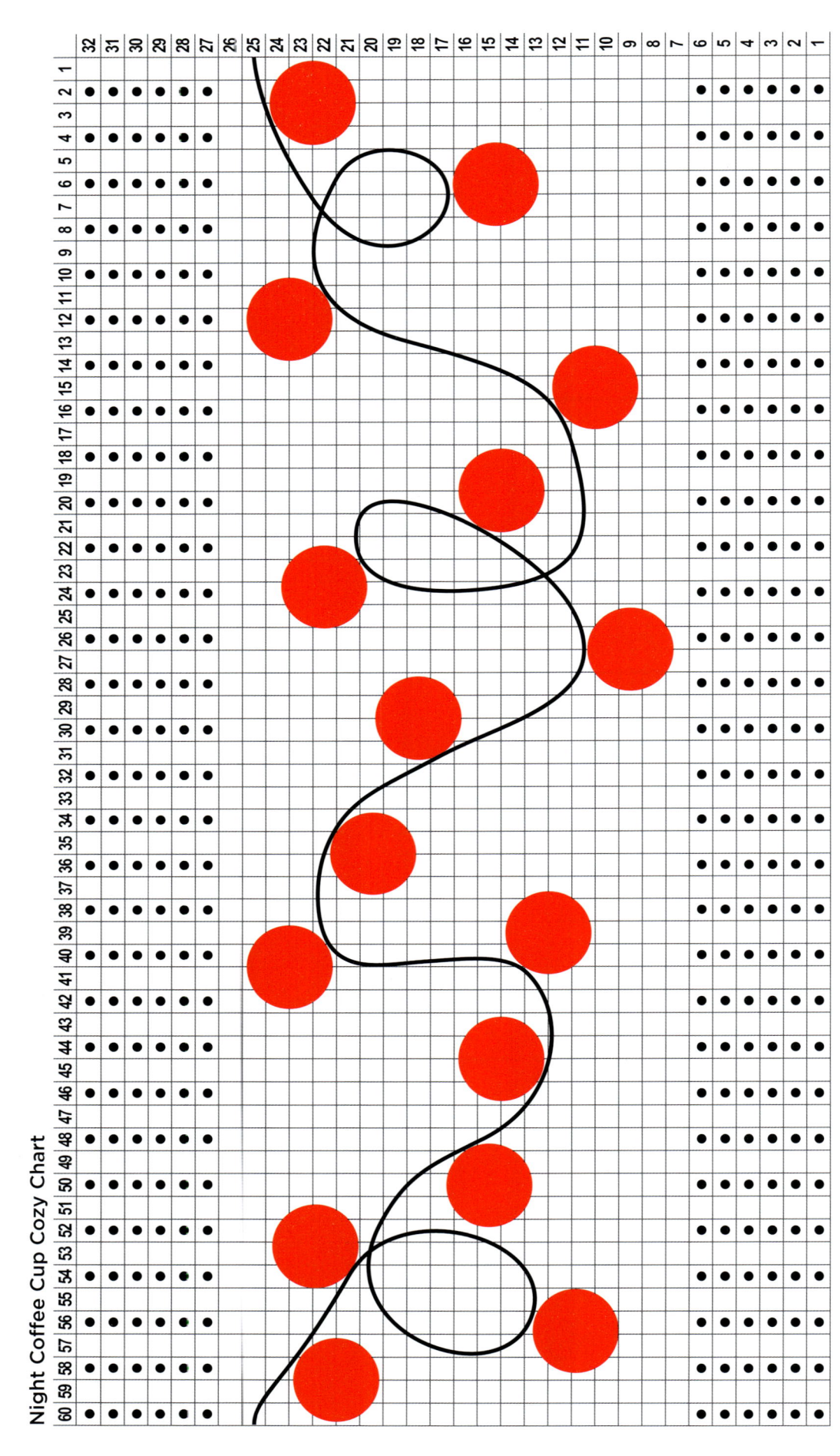

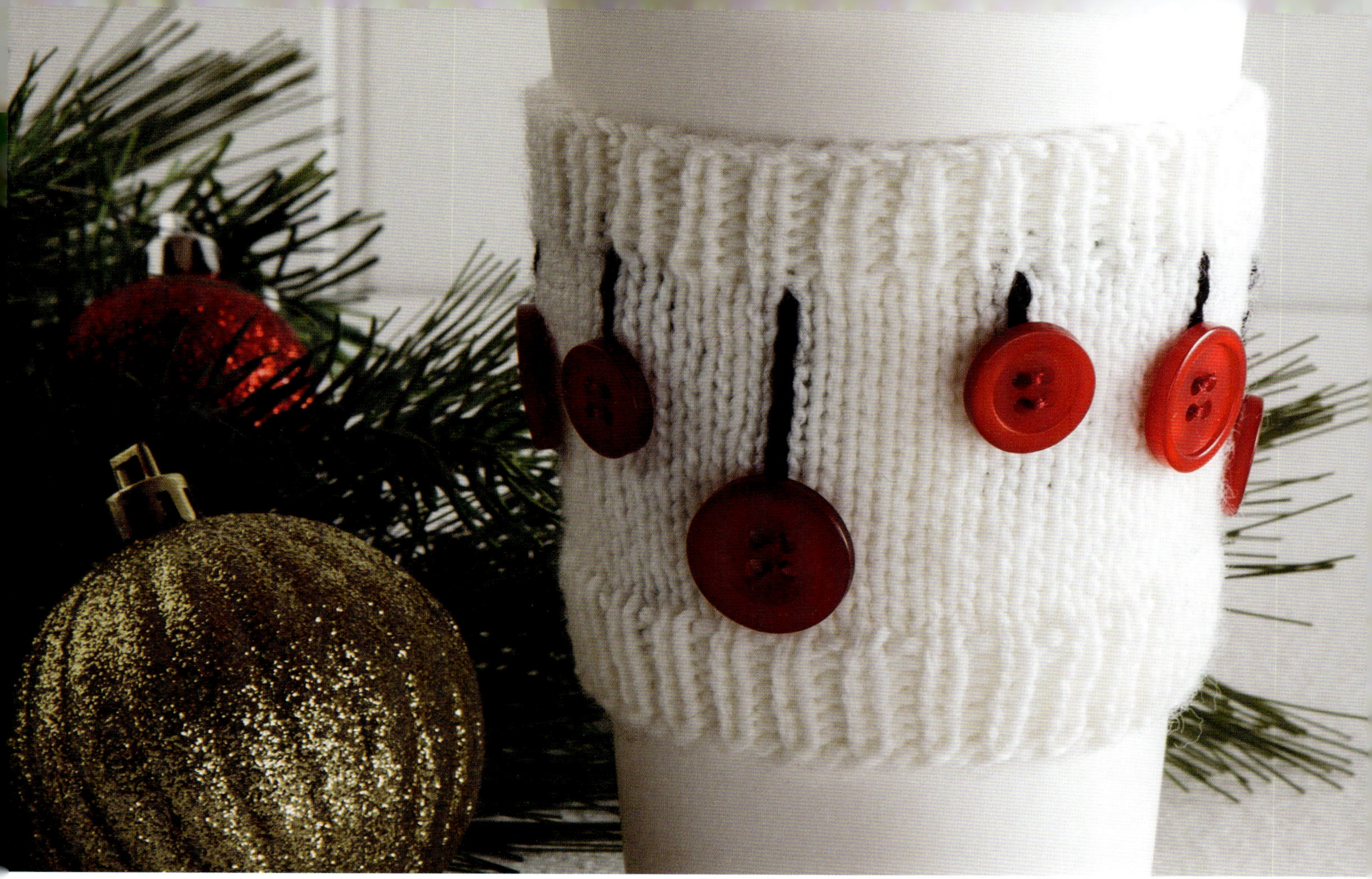

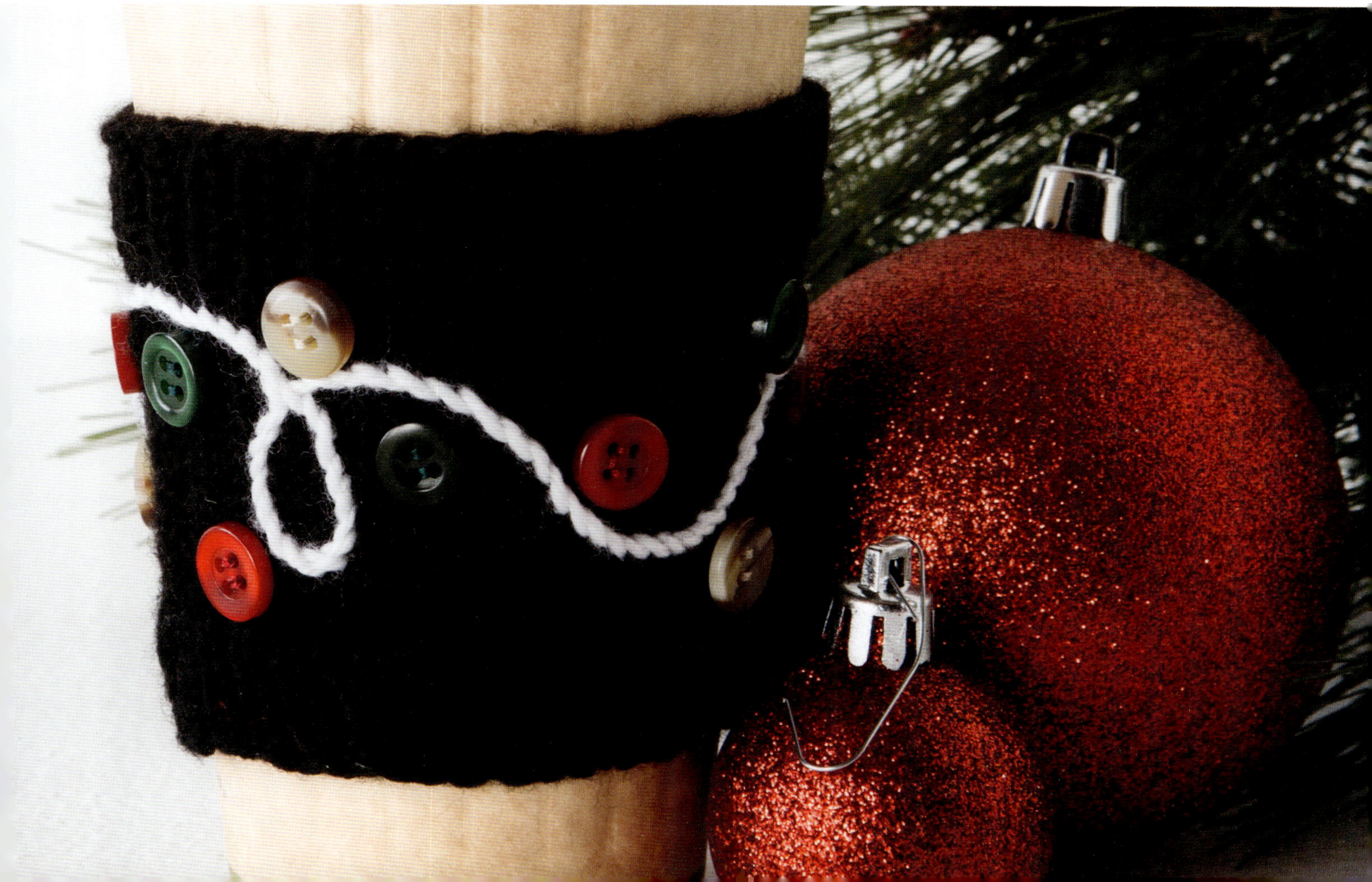

FAIR ISLE AND FESTIVE FOX PILLOWS

by Zabet Kempfert

FINISHED MEASUREMENTS

18" square.

YARN

Fair Isle Fox Pillow:

Knit Picks Wool of the Andes Sport (100% Peruvian Highland Wool; 137 yards/50g): MC White 25269, 4 balls; C1 Hollyberry 25298, 3 balls.

Festive Fox Pillow:

Knit Picks Wool of the Andes Sport (100% Peruvian Highland Wool; 137 yards/50g): MC Wonderland Heather 25287, 2 balls; C1 Pumpkin 25295, 2 balls; C2 White 25269, 1 ball; C3 Hollyberry 25298, 2 balls; C4 Coal 25268, 1 ball.

NEEDLES

US 5 (3.75mm) circular needles, or size to obtain gauge.

NOTIONS

Yarn Needle
Stitch Markers
18" Pillow Insert

GAUGE

20 sts and 21 rows = 4" in stranded St st in the round, blocked.

Notes:

This set of pillows features both the beauty and the cuteness of winter's cleverest animal. Curious foxes look out from a traditional Fair Isle pattern on the Fair Isle Fox pillow, while foxes adorned with Santa hats show their holiday spirit on the Festive Fox pillow.

Both pillows are worked in the round from the bottom up, with the same pattern on the back as on the front. Once the stitches at the top of the pillow are grafted together, a pillow insert can be placed inside, and the bottom edge is sewn shut.

DIRECTIONS

Fair Isle Fox Pillow

Loosely CO 180 sts in MC, leaving a 2-yard tail for finishing.
PM and join to work in the rnd, being careful not to twist sts.
K 2 rnds.
Join C1 and begin working from Fair Isle Fox Chart, repeating the 20 st pattern 9 times across the rnd and reading each chart row from right to left, knitting all sts. Work Rnds 1-91 once.
K 2 rnds with MC.
Break all yarns, leaving a 2-yard tail of MC. Starting at the beginning of the rnd, graft pillow closed.

Festive Fox Pillow

Loosely CO 180 sts in MC, leaving a 2-yard tail for finishing.
PM and join to work in the rnd, being careful not to twist sts.
K 1 rnd.
Join C1, C2, C3 and C4, and begin working from Festive Fox Chart, repeating the 12 st pattern 15 times across the rnd and reading each chart row from right to left, knitting all sts.
Work Rnds 1-50 two times.
K 1 rnd with MC.
Break all yarns, leaving a 2-yard tail of MC. Starting at the beginning of the rnd, graft pillow closed.

Finishing

Weave in ends, wash and block to finished measurements.
Place pillow insert into finished piece. Using the tail of MC, sew CO edge closed, making sure to match sts with the grafted sts.

Fair Isle Fox Chart

Legend

K
Knit stitch

Fair Isle Fox

MC

C1

Festive Fox

MC

C1

C2

C3

C4

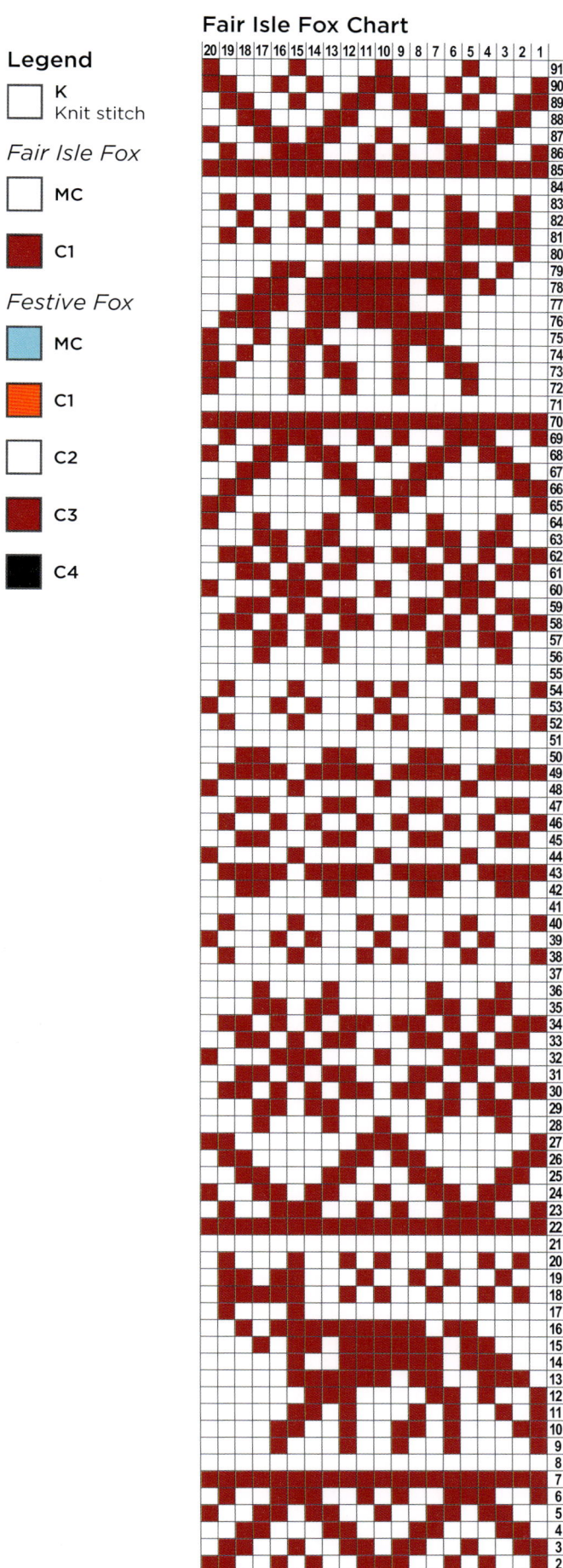

Festive Fox Chart

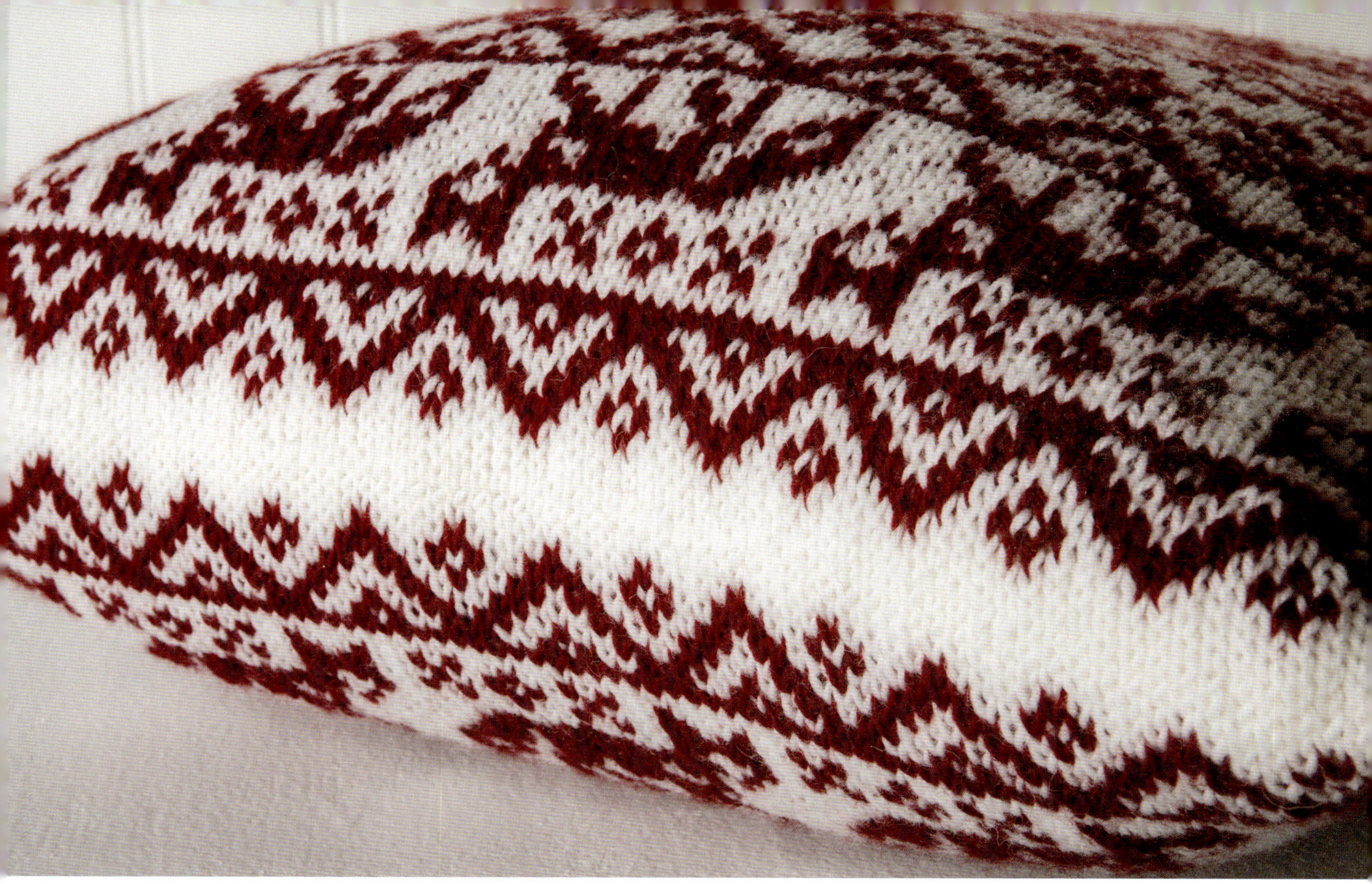

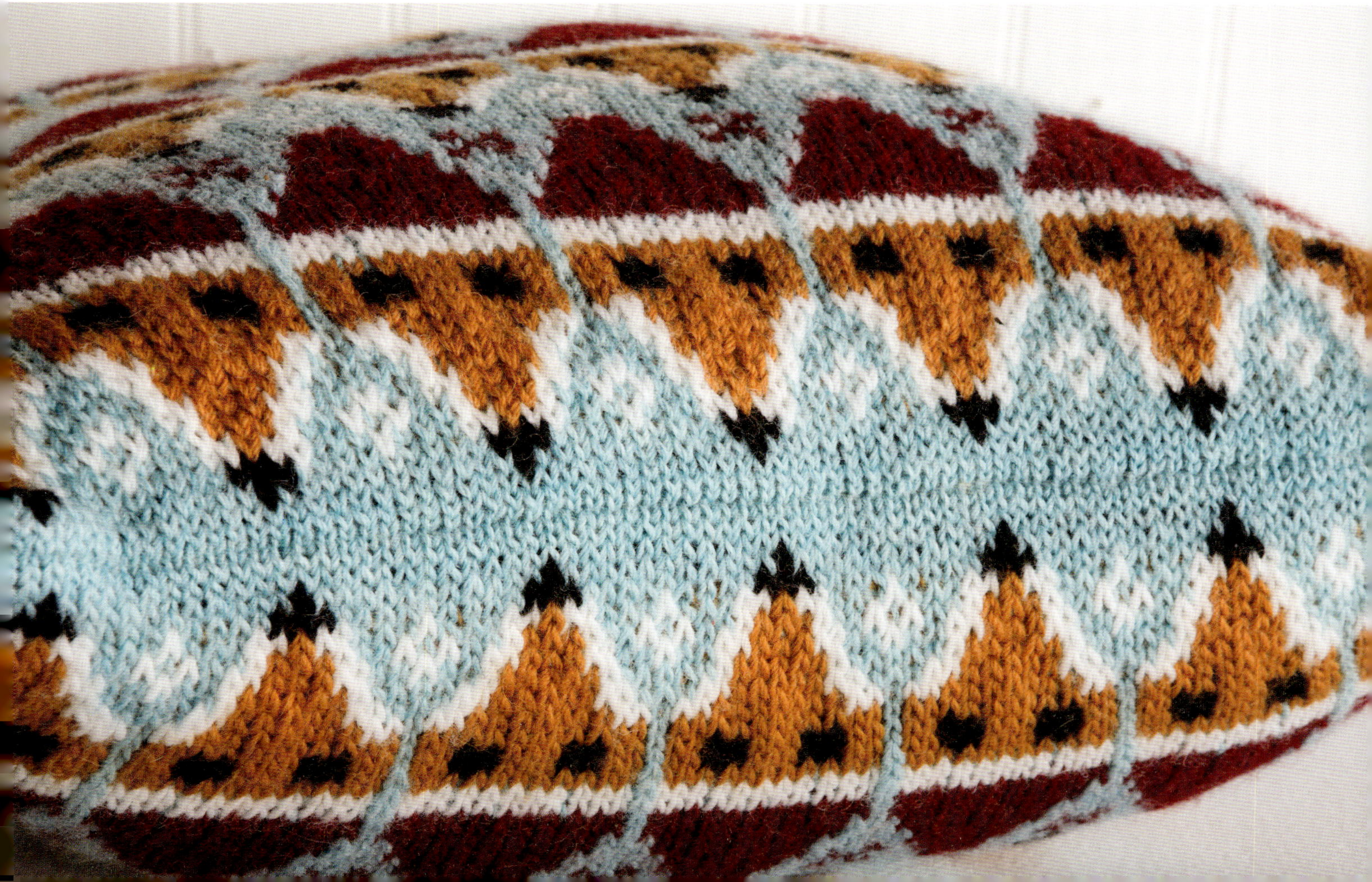

FAIR ISLE AND GEOMETRIC STOCKINGS

by Emily Kintigh

FINISHED MEASUREMENTS

7" cuff width x 19" high; hook 2" long.

YARN

Fair Isle Stocking:

Knit Picks Wool of the Andes Worsted (100% Peruvian Highland Wool; 110 yards/50g): C1 White 24065, C2 Garnet Heather 25633, 2 balls each.

Geometric Stocking:

Knit Picks Wool of the Andes Worsted (100% Peruvian Highland Wool; 110 yards/50g): C1 White 24065, C2 Garnet Heather 25633, C3 Forest Heather 23897, 2 balls each.

NEEDLES

US 4 (3.5mm) DPNs or two 24" circular needles for two circulars technique, or one 32" or longer circular needle for Magic Loop technique and DPNs, or 2 sizes below gauge needle.
US 6 (4mm) DPNs or two 24" circular needles for two circulars technique, or one 32" or longer circular needle for Magic Loop technique, or size to obtain gauge.

NOTIONS

Yarn Needle
Stitch Markers
Scrap Yarn
Spare Needles in a small size

GAUGE

28 sts and 28 rows = 4" in stranded St st in the rnd on larger needles, blocked.

For pattern support, contact
auntieemsstudio@gmail.com

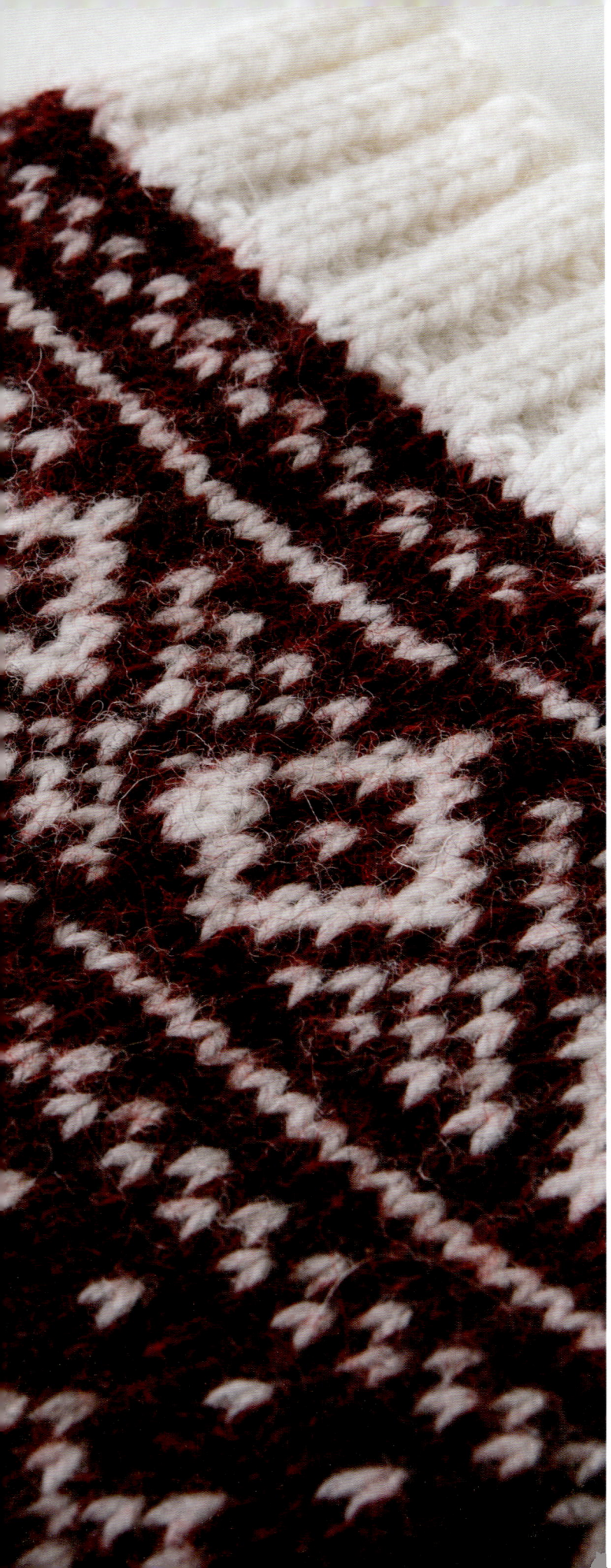

Notes:

Both stockings follow the same pattern, but use different color-work charts to make either a traditional Fair Isle or a modern geometric stocking.

The stockings are worked from the cuff down in the round. Stitches are knitted onto scrap yarn to be worked later for an afterthought heel.

For the Geometric Stocking heel, an extra section of C3 is worked just after the scrap yarn in order to make it easier to pick up stitches later for the heel.
The charts are worked in the rnd, read each row from right to left as a RS row.

2x2 Ribbing (worked in the rnd over a multiple of 4 sts)
All Rnds: (K2, P2) to end.

I-Cord

All Rows: K to end. Slide sts from left end of needle to the right bringing the yarn behind the work and pulling snuggly, creating a tube.

For a video demonstration of how to work Kitchener st, see http://tutorials.knitpicks.com/wptutorials/kitchener-stitch/

DIRECTIONS

Fair Isle Stocking
Cuff
With C1 and smaller needles, loosely CO 96 sts. PM and join in the rnd being careful not to twist the sts. Work in 2x2 Ribbing for 1.5."

Leg
Switch to larger needles. Work Rnds 1-66 of Fair Isle Chart.
Next Rnd: With scrap yarn, K48 sts. Slip 48 sts just worked back onto the LH needle. With C2, K48 sts on scrap yarn, then K48 remaining sts.

Foot
Work Rnds 28-38, then Rnds 1-27 of Fair Isle Chart. Break C2.

Toe
Rnd 1: With C1, K to end.
Rnd 2: (K14, K2tog) to end. 90 sts.
Rnd 3: K to end.
Rnd 4: (K13, K2tog) to end. 84 sts.
Rnd 5: K to end.
Rnd 6: (K12, K2tog) to end. 78 sts.
Rnd 7: K to end.
Rnd 8: (K11, K2tog) to end. 72 sts.
Rnd 9: K to end.
Rnd 10: (K10, K2tog) to end. 66 sts.
Rnd 11: K to end.
Rnd 12: (K9, K2tog) to end. 60 sts.
Rnd 13: K to end.
Rnd 14: (K8, K2tog) to end. 54 sts.
Rnd 15: (K7, K2tog) to end. 48 sts.
Rnd 16: (K6, K2tog) to end. 42 sts.
Rnd 17: (K5, K2tog) to end. 36 sts.
Rnd 18: (K4, K2tog) to end. 30 sts.
Rnd 19: (K3, K2tog) to end. 24 sts.

Rnd 20: (K2, K2tog) to end. 18 sts.
Rnd 21: (K1, K2tog) to end. 12 sts.
Rnd 22: K2tog to end. 6 sts.
Cut yarn and pull through remaining sts.

Heel

Transfer sts from scrap yarn onto larger needles. This can be done by putting a smaller needle through one side of each st along the rnd below the scrap yarn, then repeating with another needle along the rnd above. The scrap yarn can then be removed and the sts transferred to the larger needles to be worked. There should be 48 sts picked up along the bottom and 48 sts picked up along the top, for a total of 96 sts.

Rnd 1: With C1, K to end.
Rnd 2: (SSK, K44, K2tog) twice. 92 sts.
Rnd 3: K to end.
Rnd 4: (SSK, K42, K2tog) twice. 88 sts.
Rnd 5: K to end.
Rnd 6: (SSK, K40, K2tog) twice. 84 sts.
Rnd 7: K to end.
Rnd 8: (SSK, K38, K2tog) twice. 80 sts.
Rnd 9: K to end.
Rnd 10: (SSK, K36, K2tog) twice. 76 sts.
Rnd 11: K to end.
Rnd 12: (SSK, K34, K2tog) twice. 72 sts.
Rnd 13: (SSK, K32, K2tog) twice. 68 sts.
Rnd 14: (SSK, K30, K2tog) twice. 64 sts.
Rnd 15: (SSK, K28, K2tog) twice. 60 sts.
Rnd 16: (SSK, K26, K2tog) twice. 56 sts.
Rnd 17: (SSK, K24, K2tog) twice. 52 sts.
Rnd 18: (SSK, K22, K2tog) twice. 48 sts.
Cut yarn leaving a long tail. Place half of the sts on one needle and the other half on another and use Kitchener stitch to seam heel.

Geometric Stocking

Cuff

With C1 and smaller needles, loosely CO 96 sts. PM and join in the rnd being careful not to twist the sts. Work in 2x2 Ribbing for 1.5."

Leg

Switch to larger needles. Work Rnds 1-9 of Geometric Chart 7 times, then Rnds 1-3 once more.

Next Rnd: With scrap yarn, K48 sts. Slip 48 sts just worked back onto the LH needle. With C3, K48 sts, cut yarn. Slip 48 sts just worked back onto the LH needle. Rejoin C3 and work Rnd 4 of Geometric Chart across 48 sts on scrap yarn, then across 48 remaining sts.

Foot

Work Rnds 5-9 of Geometric Chart, then Rnds 1-9 another 3 times, then Rnds 1-6 once more. Break C1 and C3.

Toe

Follow directions for Fair Isle Stocking Toe, using C2 instead of C1.

Heel

Follow directions for Fair Isle Stocking Heel, using C3 instead of C1.

Finishing

Weave in ends, making sure to close up any holes formed at the corners of the heel.

Loop

With C1 and smaller DPNs, CO 3 sts. Work in I-cord until piece measures 7". BO all sts.
Securely sew the loop to the cuff, forming a 2" loop. Wash and block.

Geometric Chart

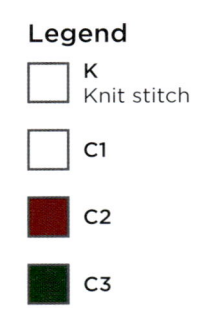

Legend

- ☐ **K** Knit stitch
- ☐ **C1**
- ■ **C2**
- ■ **C3**

> " Christmas
> is doing a
> little something
> extra for
> someone. "

- Charles M. Shulz

Fair Isle Chart

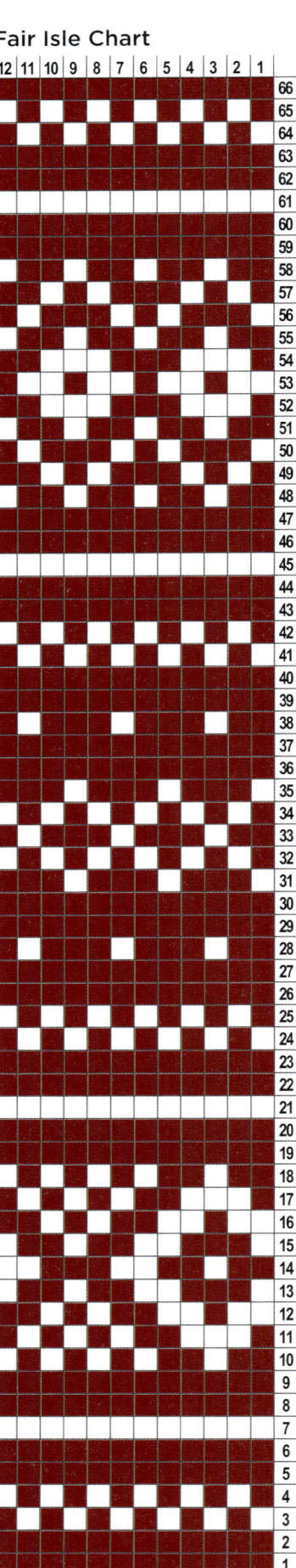

HOLIDAY CARD HOLDERS

by Quenna Lee

FINISHED MEASUREMENTS

Snowflake: 3.25" opening x 5" high.
Ho Ho Ho: 3.75" opening x 5" high.

YARN

Knit Picks Stroll Glimmer
(70% Fine Superwash Merino, 25%
Nylon, 5% Stellina; 231 yards/50g):
MC White 25493, C1 Peacock 25485,
C2 Frost 25495, one ball each.

NEEDLES

US 6 (4mm) DPNs or two 24" circular
needles for two circulars technique, or one
32" or longer circular needle for Magic
Loop technique, or size to obtain gauge.

NOTIONS

US G (4mm) Crochet Hook
Two 0.5" Buttons
Yarn Needle
Stitch Marker

GAUGE

24 sts and 28 rows = 4" in stranded St st
in the rnd, blocked.

For pattern support, contact
blissfulbyquenna@yahoo.com

Notes:

Card holders are worked in the round from the bottom up. After BO, the button loop is formed with a crochet hook. Separate directions are given for each holder.

Charts are worked in the round; read each row from right to left.

For Snowflake version only:

With MC, CO 40 sts. PM and join to work in the rnd, being careful not to twist sts.

Rnds 1-5: K. Join C1.

Rnds 6-30: Work Rnds 1-25 of Snowflake Chart, rep chart two times across the rnd, alternating MC and C1 as directed. Cut C1.

Rnds 31-33: With MC, K.

Rnds 34-35: *K1, P1; rep from * to end.

Remove M, work next 9 sts in K1, P1 pattern. BO in pattern until 1 st remains. Switch to crochet hook and insert it at the beginning of BO and pull yarn through last st, leaving a single loop on hook. Work single chain until it measures 1.5". Pull yarn through the base of chain, forming a button loop.

For Ho Ho Ho version only:

With C2, CO 44 sts. PM and join to work in the rnd being careful not to twist sts.

Rnds 1-14: K. Join C1.

Rnds 15-21: Work Rnds 1-7 of Ho Ho Ho Chart, rep chart four times across the rnd, switching to MC as directed. Cut C2 and C1.

Rnds 22-33: With MC, K.

Rnds 34-35: *K1, P1; rep from * to end.

Remove M, work next 11 sts in K1, P1 pattern. BO in pattern until 1 st remains. Switch to crochet hook and insert it at the beginning of BO and pull yarn through last st, leaving a single loop on hook. Work single chain until it measures 1.5". Pull yarn through the base of chain, forming a button loop.

Finishing (for both versions)

On the RS, sew button near top opening, opposite button loop. With RS facing each other, sew bottom CO opening together.

Weave in ends, wash and block to measurements.

Snowflake Chart

20	19	18	17	16	15	14	13	12	11	10	9	8	7	6	5	4	3	2	1	
																				25
																				24
																				23
																				22
																				21
																				20
																				19
																				18
																				17
																				16
																				15
																				14
																				13
																				12
																				11
																				10
																				9
																				8
																				7
																				6
																				5
																				4
																				3
																				2
																				1

Ho Ho Ho Chart

Legend

K
Knit stitch

MC

C1

C2

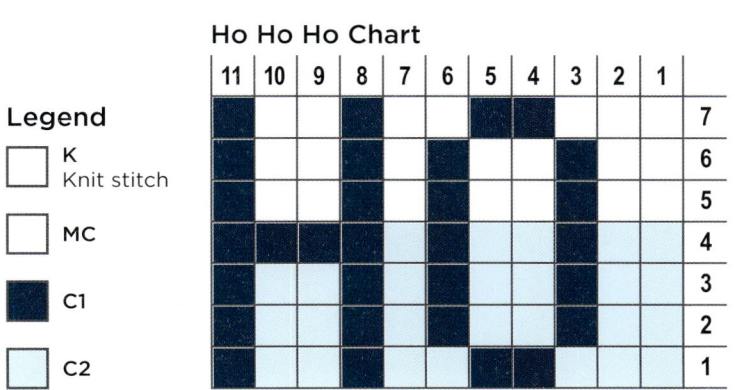

MAIN ATTRACTION STOCKINGS

by Rebecca Minner

FINISHED MEASUREMENTS

7" wide x 24" long from cuff to toe.

YARN

Patterned stocking:

Knit Picks Palette

(100% Peruvian Highland Wool; 231 yards/50g): MC White 23728, C1 Aurora Heather 25537; 2 balls each.

Striped stocking:

Knit Picks Wool of the Andes Superwash Bulky

(100% Superwash Wool; 137 yards/100g): MC White 26522, C1 Aurora Heather 26494; 2 skeins each.

NEEDLES

US 3 (3.25mm) 16" circular needles plus DPNs, or size to obtain gauge.
US 10.5 (6.5mm) 16" circular needles plus DPNs, or size to obtain gauge.

NOTIONS

Yarn Needle
4 Stitch Markers, 1 different from the other 3
Smooth Scrap Yarn

GAUGE

16 sts and 18.5 rows = 4" in St st using bulky yarn on larger needles in the rnd, blocked.

32 sts and 33 rows = 4" over colorwork chart using fingering yarn on smaller needles in the rnd, blocked.

Notes:

When it comes to stockings, there seems to be people who do stockings and people that do STOCKINGS. People that say that's the best thing to open on Christmas morning. People that start collecting stocking stuffers in January. People that have a disregard for traditional stocking stuffers and need a little more room for all of that loot. People that need a serious stocking - like these. One is more traditional and a labor of love, with stripe after stripe of colorwork and a place to knit or embroider a name for an instant heirloom. The other is more likely to be the choice if you need it right away, or need to make more than one before the big day, as it's worked up quickly in a bulky yarn. They can be as colorful as you like with each stripe of the bulky stocking and each stripe of colorwork a different color, or they could stay two-tone for simplicity's sake.

When knitting colorwork stretches over five stitches long, anchor the float by twisting it with the working yarn to avoid excessive loops that goodies and fingers may snag on the inside. The charts are worked in the rnd; read each row from right to left as a RS row, knitting all sts.

Optional Eyelet: Immediately following the Cuff but before beginning the Leg, a row of eyelets may be worked to weave a ribbon or I-cord through to keep the stocking contents from spilling out.
Rnd 1: (YO, K2tog) around.
Rnd 2: K.

If you would like to stitch a name or initials on either stocking, simply omit the Tree Chart from the patterned fingering stocking and work those rnds in St st, or make the first C1 stripe on the striped bulky stocking wide enough to accommodate the lettering. Stitch the name in as you knit or duplicate stitch or embroider it after you finish the stockings.

For a video demonstration of how to work Kitchener st, see http://tutorials.knitpicks.com/wptutorials/kitchener-stitch/

Tree Chart (worked in the rnd over 14 sts)
Rnd 1: K14 with C1.
Rnd 2: (K6 with C1, K1 with MC) 2 times.
Rnd 3: (K1 MC, K4 C1, K1 MC, K1 C1) 2 times.
Rnd 4: K1 C1, K1 MC, K2 C1, (K1 MC, K1 C1) 2 times, (K1 MC, K2 C1) 2 times.
Rnd 5: (K1 MC, K2 C1) 4 times, K1 MC, K1 C1.
Rnd 6: K2 C1, K9 MC, K2 C1, K1 MC.
Rnd 7: K1 C1, K2 MC, K2 C1, K1 MC, K1 C1, K1 MC, K2 C1, K2 MC, K2 C1.
Rnd 8: (K1 MC, K1 C1) 2 times, K1 MC, K3 C1, (K1 MC, K1 C1) 3 times.
Rnd 9: (K2 C1, K2 MC, K2 C1, K1 MC) 2 times.
Rnd 10: K3 MC, K3 C1, K1 MC, K3 C1, K4 MC.
Rnd 11: (K1 C1, K1 MC, K3 C1, K1 MC) 2 times, K2 C1.
Rnd 12: (K1 MC, K5 C1) 2 times, K1 MC, K1 C1.

Rnd 13: K4 C1, (K1 MC, K1 C1) 2 times, K1 MC, K4 C1, K1 MC.
Rnd 14: Rep Rnd 11.
Rnd 15: K3 C1, K1 MC, (K2 C1, K1 MC) 2 times, K3 C1, K1 MC.
Rnd 16: K1 MC, K3 C1, (K1 MC, K1 C1) 2 times, K1 MC, K3 C1, K1 MC, K1 C1.
Rnd 17: (K2 C1, K1 MC) 2 times, K1 C1, K1 MC, (K2 C1, K1 MC) 2 times.
Rnd 18: K3 C1, K1 MC, (K2 C1, K1 MC) 2 times, K4 C1.
Rnd 19: Rep Rnd 4.
Rnd 20: (K2 C1, K1 MC) 2 times, K1 C1, K1 MC, K2 C1, K1 MC, K3 C1.
Rnd 21: Rep Rnd 5.
Rnd 22: Rep Rnd 4.
Rnd 23: Rep Rnd 20.
Rnd 24: Rep Rnd 15.
Rnd 25: Rep Rnd 16.
Rnd 26: Rep Rnd 11.
Rnd 27: Rep Rnd 12.
Rnd 28: Rep Rnd 2.
Rnd 29: Rep Rnd 1.

Heart Chart (worked in the rnd over 14 sts)
Rnd 1: K14 with MC.
Rnd 2: K2 with MC, (K1 with C1, K3 with MC) 2 times, K1 with C1, K2 with MC, K1 with C1.
Rnd 3: (K1 C1, K4 MC, K1 C1, K1 MC) 2 times.
Rnd 4: K1 MC, (K1 C1, K2 MC) 2 times, K1 MC, (K1 C1, K2 MC) 2 times.
Rnd 5: (K2 MC, K1 C1) 2 times, K1 MC, (K1 C1, K2 MC) 2 times, K1 C1.
Rnd 6: (K1 C1, K2 MC) 4 times, K1 C1, K1 MC.
Rnd 7: K4 MC, K1 C1, K3 MC, K1 C1, K4 MC, K1 C1.
Rnd 8: K1 MC, K2 C1, K2 MC, K1 C1, K1 MC, K1 C1, K2 MC, K2 C1, K2 MC.
Rnd 9: K4 C1, K2 MC, K1 C1, K2 MC, K4 C1, K1 MC.
Rnd 10: K1 C1, K1 MC, K3 C1, K3 MC, K3 C1, K1 MC, K2 C1.
Rnd 11: K1 MC, K1 C1, K1 MC, (K2 C1, K1 MC, K1 C1, K1 MC) 2 times, K1 C1.
Rnd 12: K1 C1, K1 MC, K3 C1, K3 MC, K3 C1, K1 MC, K1 C1, K1 MC.
Rnd 13: K1 MC, K3 C1, K2 MC, K1 C1, K2 MC, K3 C1, K1 MC, K1 C1.
Rnd 14: K3 C1, K2 MC, K1 C1, K1 MC, K1 C1, K2 MC, K3 C1, K1 MC.
Rnd 15: K2 C1, K2 MC, K1 C1, K3 MC, K1 C1, K2 MC, K3 C1.
Rnd 16: (K1 C1, K2 MC) 4 times, K2 C1.
Rnd 17: Rep Rnd 5.
Rnd 18: Rep Rnd 4.
Rnd 19: Rep Rnd 3.
Rnd 20: Rep Rnd 2.
Rnd 21: Rep Rnd 1.

Snowflake Chart (worked in the rnd over 14 sts)
Rnd 1: K14 with C1.
Rnd 2: K2 with C1, K1 with MC, K7 with C1, K1 with MC, K2 with C1, K1 with MC.
Rnd 3: K1 C1, K1 MC, K9 C1, K1 MC, K2 C1.

Rnd 4: K1 MC, K2 C1, K7 MC, K2 C1, K1 MC, K1 C1.
Rnd 5: K2 C1, K1 MC, K7 C1, K1 MC, K2 C1, K1 MC.
Rnd 6: (K1 C1, K1 MC, K3 C1, K1 MC) 2 times, K2 C1.
Rnd 7: (K1 MC, K2 C1) 4 times, K1 MC, K1 C1.
Rnd 8: (K2 C1, K2 MC, K2 C1, K1 MC) 2 times.
Rnd 9: K4 C1, (K1 MC, K1 C1) 2 times, K1 MC, K4 C1, K1 MC.
Rnd 10: K1 C1, K1 MC, K3 C1, K3 MC, K3 C1, K1 M1, K1 C1, K1 MC.
Rnd 11: K2 C1, K4 MC, K1 C1, K4 MC, K2 C1, K1 MC.
Rnd 12: Rep Rnd 10.
Rnd 13: Rep Rnd 9.
Rnd 14: Rep Rnd 8.
Rnd 15: Rep Rnd 7.
Rnd 16: Rep Rnd 6.
Rnd 17: Rep Rnd 5.
Rnd 18: Rep Rnd 4.
Rnd 19: Rep Rnd 3.
Rnd 20: Rep Rnd 2.
Rnd 21: Rep Rnd 1.

Star Chart (worked in the rnd over 14 sts)
Rnd 1: K14 with MC.
Rnd 2: K1 with MC, K3 with C1, K2 with MC, K1 with C1, K2 with MC, K3 with C1, K2 with MC.
Rnd 3: (K2 MC, K1 C1) 2 times, K1 MC, (K1 C1, K2 MC) 2 times, K1 C1.
Rnd 4: (K1 C1, K3 MC) 3 times, K1 C1, K1 MC.
Rnd 5: (K1 MC, K1 C1) 2 times, (K2 MC, K1 C1) 2 times, K1 MC, K1 C1, K2 MC.
Rnd 6: K2 MC, K1 C1, K2 MC, K3 C1, (K2 MC, K1 C1) 2 times.
Rnd 7: (K1 MC, K1 C1) 2 times, (K2 MC, K1 C1) 2 times, K1 MC, K1 C1, K2 MC.
Rnd 8: (K1 C1, K3 MC) 3 times, K1 C1, K1 MC.
Rnd 9: (K2 MC, K1 C1) 2 times, K1 MC, (K1 C1, K2 MC) 2 times, K1 C1.
Rnd 10: K1 MC, K2 C1, K3 MC, K1 C1, K3 MC, K2 C1, K2 MC.
Rnd 11: K3 C1, K7 MC, K3 C1, K1 MC.
Rnd 12: K2 C1, K1 MC, (K3 C1, K1 MC) 2 times, K2 C1, K1 MC.
Rnd 13: K1 C1, K1 MC, K3 C1, K3 MC, K3 C1, K1 MC, K1 C1, K1 MC.
Rnd 14: K1 MC, K3 C1, K2 MC, K1 C1, K2 MC, K3 C1, K1 MC, K1 C1.
Rnd 15: (K1 C1, K4 MC, K1 C1, K1 MC) 2 times.
Rnd 16: Rep Rnd 14.
Rnd 17: Rep Rnd 13.
Rnd 18: Rep Rnd 12.
Rnd 19: Rep Rnd 11.
Rnd 20: Rep Rnd 10.
Rnd 21: Rep Rnd 9.
Rnd 22: Rep Rnd 8.
Rnd 23: Rep Rnd 7.
Rnd 24: Rep Rnd 6.
Rnd 25: Rep Rnd 5.
Rnd 26: Rep Rnd 4.
Rnd 27: Rep Rnd 3.
Rnd 28: Rep Rnd 2.
Rnd 29: Rep Rnd 1.

DIRECTIONS

Fingering Patterned Stocking

Cuff

Using MC and smaller needles with fingering yarn, loosely CO 112 sts. Being careful not to twist, PM, join for working in the rnd.

Rnds 1 and 3: P.

Rnd 2: K.

Rnds 4-11: (P1 with MC, K1 with C1) to end.

Rnds 12 and 13: Using MC, K.

Work Optional Eyelet over 2 additional rnds if desired.

Leg

Each chart row is worked 8 times across the rnd. Knit all rows of the Tree Chart, Heart Chart, Snowflake Chart, and then Star Chart once, or in order as desired. Break yarn.

To set up for afterthought heel, Sl the last 28 sts just worked back onto the LH needle. Using scrap yarn, K these 28 once again, SM, K28. Sl the last 28 sts just worked back onto the LH needle.
Rejoin MC and C1 and work Tree Chart and Heart Chart. Break C1 yarn.

Toe

Set Up Rnd: Using MC, K28, PM, K56, PM, K28. 112 sts.

Rnd 1: K to 3 sts before M, K2tog, K1, SM, K1, SSK, K to 3 sts before M, K2tog, K1, SM, K1, SSK, K to end. 4 sts dec.

Rnd 2: K.

Rep Rnds 1-2 18 more times, switching to DPNs when necessary. 36 sts.

Rep Rnd 1 once more. 32 sts. K the 8 sts to next M. Break yarn and Kitchener st remaining sts of toe closed.

Heel

Return sts to smaller needles and remove scrap yarn. 112 sts.

Set Up Rnd: Using MC, PU 1 st in gap, K56, PU 1 st in gap, PM, PU 1 st in gap, K56, PU 1 st in gap, PM for beginning of rnd. 116 sts.

Set Up Dec Rnd 1: K1, SSK, K52, K2tog, K1, SM, K1, SSK, K52, K2tog, K1. 112 sts.

Rnd 1: K1, SSK, K to 3 sts before M, K2tog, K1, SM, K1, SSK, K to 3 sts before M, K2tog, K1. 4 sts dec.

Rnd 2: K.

Rep Rnds 1-2 14 more times, switching to DPNs when necessary. 52 sts. Rep Rnd 1 once more. 48 sts. Break yarn

and Kitchener remaining sts of heel closed.

Bulky Striped Stocking

Cuff

Using MC and larger needles with bulky yarn, loosely CO 56 sts. Being careful not to twist, PM, join for working in the rnd.

Rnd 1: P.

Rnd 2: K.

Rep Rnds 1-2 3 more times, rep Rnd 1 once more.

Work Optional Eyelet over 2 additional rnds if desired.

Leg

Rnds 1-5: Using C1, K.

Rnds 6-10: Using MC, K.

Rep Rnds 1-10 5 more times. Break yarn.

To set up for heel, Sl the last 14 sts just worked back onto the LH needle. Using scrap yarn, K these 14 once again, SM, K 14. Sl the last 14 sts just worked back onto the LH needle.
Rejoin MC and C1 and work Rnds 1-10 2 times. Rep Rnds 1-5 once more. Break C1 yarn.

Toe

Set Up Rnd: Using MC, K14, PM, K28, PM, K14. 56 sts.

Rnd 1: K to 3 sts before M, K2tog, K1, SM, K1, SSK, K to 3 sts before M, K2tog, K1, SM, K1, SSK, K to end. 4 sts dec.

Rnd 2: K.

Rep Rnds 1-2 8 more times, switching to DPNs when necessary. 20 sts. Rep Rnd 1 once more. 16 sts. K the 4 sts to M. Break yarn and Kitchener st remaining sts of toe closed.

Heel

Return sts to larger needles and remove scrap yarn. 56 sts.

Set Up Rnd: Using MC, PU 1 st in gap, K28, PU 1 st in gap, PM, PU 1 st in gap, K28, PU 1 st in gap, PM for beginning of rnd. 60 sts.

Set Up Dec Rnd 1: K1, SSK, K24, K2tog, K1, SM, K1, SSK, K24, K2 tog, K1. 56 sts.

Rnd 1: K1, SSK, K to 3 sts before M, K2tog, K1, SM, K1, SSK, K to 3 sts before M, K2tog, K1. 4 sts dec.

Rnd 2: K.

Rep Rnds 1-2 6 more times, switching to DPNs when necessary. 28 sts. Rep Rnd 1 once more. 24 sts. Break yarn and Kitchener remaining sts of heel closed.

Finishing

Weave in ends.

Legend

- K — Knit stitch (white square)
- MC (white square)
- C1 (black square)

Tree Chart

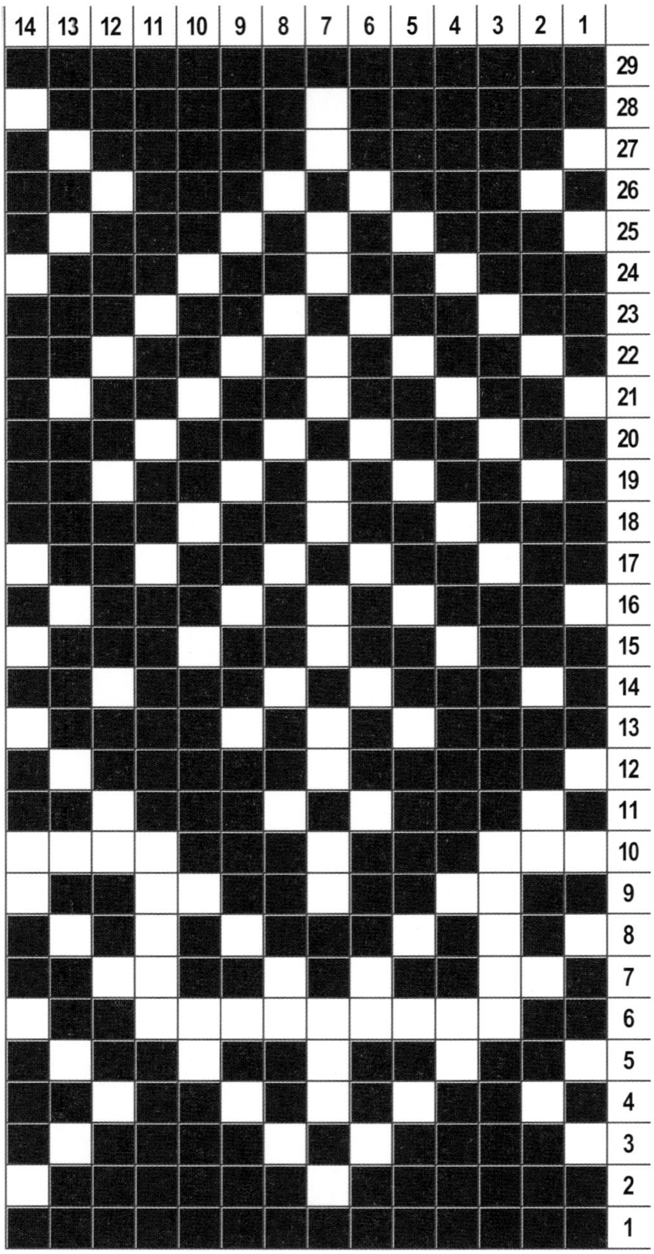

14 13 12 11 10 9 8 7 6 5 4 3 2 1
29 28 27 26 25 24 23 22 21 20 19 18 17 16 15 14 13 12 11 10 9 8 7 6 5 4 3 2 1

Heart Chart

Snowflake Chart

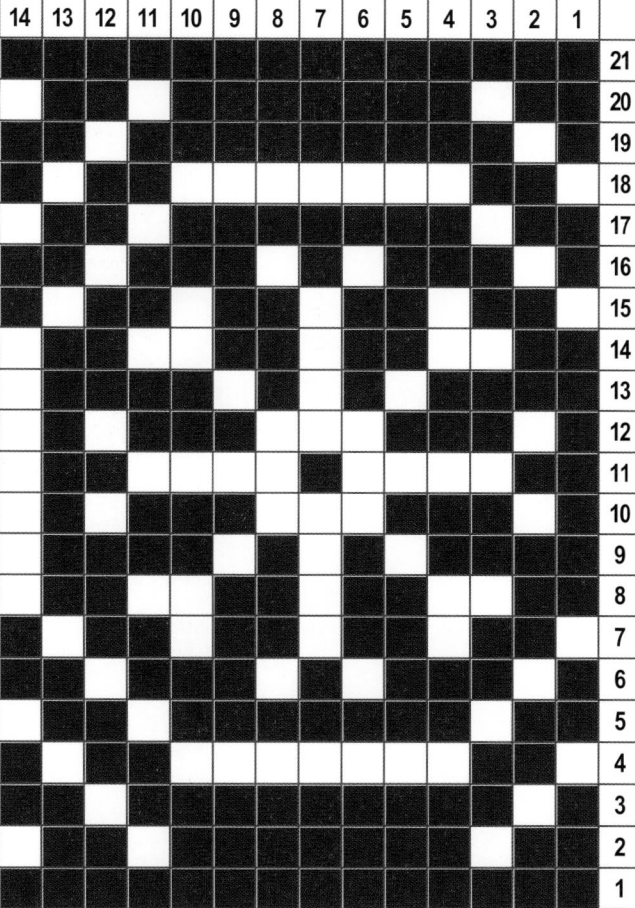

Star Chart

14	13	12	11	10	9	8	7	6	5	4	3	2	1	
														29
		■	■	■			■			■	■	■		28
■			■			■		■			■			27
	■				■				■				■	26
		■					■			■		■		25
■			■				■	■			■			24
		■		■			■				■	■		23
	■				■			■					■	22
■			■			■		■			■			21
		■				■				■		■		20
	■	■								■		■		19
	■			■	■	■		■	■	■		■		18
	■	■		■					■	■			■	17
■		■	■				■		■	■				16
	■					■		■					■	15
■		■					■		■	■				14
	■			■	■				■	■	■		■	13
	■	■		■	■		■	■		■	■			12
	■	■								■	■			11
		■					■			■	■			10
■			■			■		■						9
	■				■			■			■		■	8
		■		■			■			■		■		7
■			■			■	■	■			■			6
		■		■			■			■		■		5
	■				■				■				■	4
■			■			■		■			■			3
		■	■	■			■			■	■	■		2
														1

NAUGHTY OR NICE GIFT CARD HOLDERS

by Kathy Lewinski

FINISHED MEASUREMENTS
3.75" wide x 2.5" tall with a 1.5" flap.

YARN
Knit Picks Palette
(100% Peruvian Highland Wool;
231 yards/50g): MC Hollyberry
25539, C1 White 23728, 1 ball each.

NEEDLES
US 1 (2.25mm) DPNs or two 24"
circular needles for two circulars
technique, or one 32" or longer
circular needle for Magic Loop
technique, or size to obtain gauge.

NOTIONS
Yarn Needle
Stitch Markers
0.25" Button
Matching Sewing Thread
Sewing Needle

GAUGE
40 sts and 48 rows = 4" in stranded St st
in the round, blocked.

For pattern support, contact
jcraftyenough@gmail.com

Notes:

These fun gift card holders are knit in one piece with only one seam at the bottom. The pocket of the holder is knit in the round and then the flap is knit flat after binding off half the stitches.

This is a great scrap project as one holder uses approximately 7g/35 yards of the MC and 2g/10 yards of C1.

When a yarn needs to be carried for a length of more than four stitches behind the work, twist the MC and C1 every fourth stitch. Make sure to maintain a proper tension without pulling the floats too tightly.

When working the chart, read each row from right to left as a RS row.

DIRECTIONS

CO 74 sts with MC, leaving an 18" tail for seaming. Join together to work in the rnd being careful not to twist sts. PM between the last and first st to mark beginning of rnd.

Rnds 1 – 10: K.

Rnds 11 – 21: K with both MC and C1 following either the Naughty or Nice Chart, breaking C1 after final chart row.

Rnds 22 – 26: K with MC.

Rnd 27: P37, K37.

Rnd 28: K.

Rnds 29-30: Rep Rnds 27-28.

Rnd 31: BO 37 sts, P36. 37 sts.

Flap

The flap is worked flat.

Row 1 (WS): P.

Row 2 (RS): SSK, K until last 2 sts, K2tog. 35 sts.

Row 3: P2tog, P until last 2 sts, SSP. 33 sts.

Rep Rows 2 and 3 six times, until 9 sts remain.

Next Row: SSK, K2, YO, K2tog, K1, K2tog. 7 sts.

Next Row: P2tog, P3, SSP. 5 sts.

Next Row: SSK, K1, K2tog. 3 sts.

Next Row: P2tog, Sl1 back to left needle, SSP. 1 st.

Cut a tail, weave through last st and pull tight.

Finishing

Weave in ends. Seam the bottom using the CO tail.
Block to Finished Measurements.
Sew button in place with matching thread.

Naughty Chart

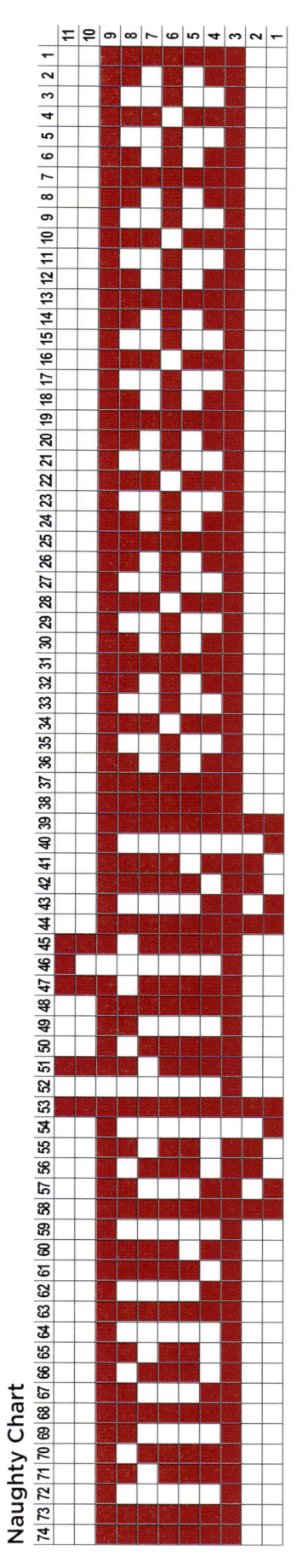

Nice Chart

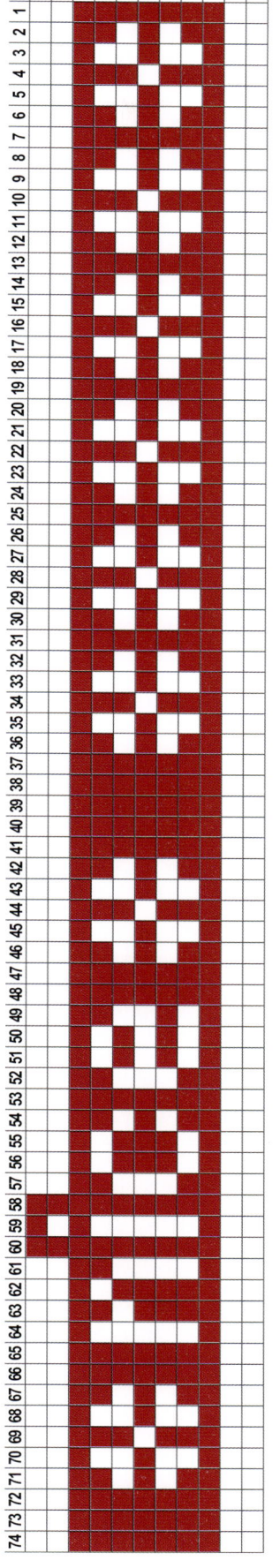

Legend

K
Knit stitch

 MC

C1

SNOWY CUSHIONS

by Claire Slade

FINISHED MEASUREMENTS

14" square.

YARN

Knit Picks Wool of the Andes Sport (100% Peruvian Highland Wool; 137 yards/50g): MC White 25269, 4 balls; C1 Hollyberry 25298, 3 balls; C2 Wonderland Heather 25287, 3 balls; C3 Pumpkin 25295, 1 ball.

NEEDLES

US 4 (3.5mm) 24" circular needles, or size to obtain gauge.

NOTIONS

Stitch marker
Yarn Needle
14" square pillow form

GAUGE

23 sts and 26 rows = 4" in stranded St st in the round, lightly blocked.

For pattern support, contact
verilyknits@gmail.com

Notes:
Both snowy pillows are knit in the round in one piece. On completion, a pillow form is inserted and both top and bottom seams are sewn up. The snowmen's noses can be knit or added afterwards using duplicate stitch.

Choose from either the traditional Scandinavian inspired snowflowers or the fun and modern snowmen to have snowy pillow gifts for all the family.

When working the charts, read all rows from right to left, as RS rows.

DIRECTIONS

Snowflowers Pillow
Using C1 CO 176 sts. PM, join to work in the rnd being careful not to twist.
Knit 3 rnds.
Join MC and work Rnds 1-16 of Snowflower Chart 5 times, then Rnds 1-13 once more.
Break MC.
Using C1 knit 3 rnds.
BO all sts.

Snowmen Pillow
Using C2 CO 168 sts. PM, join to work in the rnd being careful not to twist.
Knit 4 rnds.
Join MC and work Rnd 1 of Snowmen Chart A once.
Work Rnds 1-24 of Snowmen Chart B 3 times, then Rnds 1-11 once more.
Work Rnd 1 of Snowmen Chart C once.
Break MC.
Using C2 knit 4 rnds.
BO all sts.

Finishing
Weave in ends, wash and block lightly, being careful not to overstretch.
Sew the bottom seam, insert the pillow form and then sew the upper seam.

Snowflowers Chart

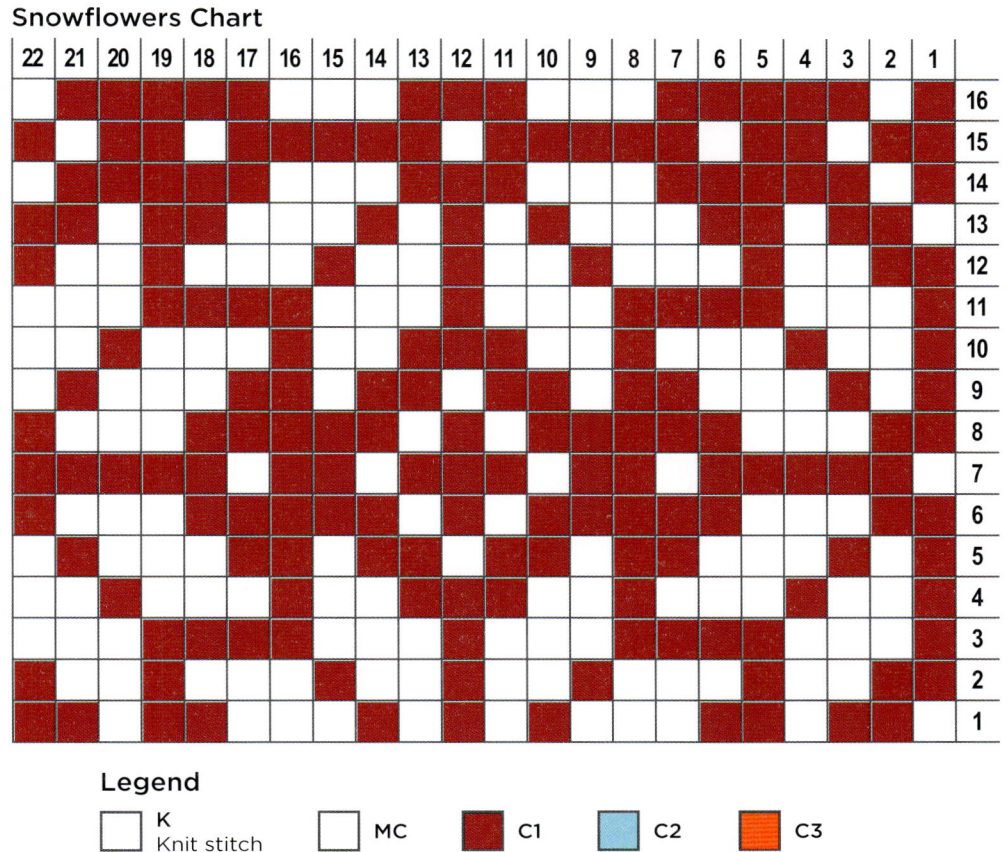

22 21 20 19 18 17 16 15 14 13 12 11 10 9 8 7 6 5 4 3 2 1
16 15 14 13 12 11 10 9 8 7 6 5 4 3 2 1

Legend

- K Knit stitch
- MC
- C1
- C2
- C3

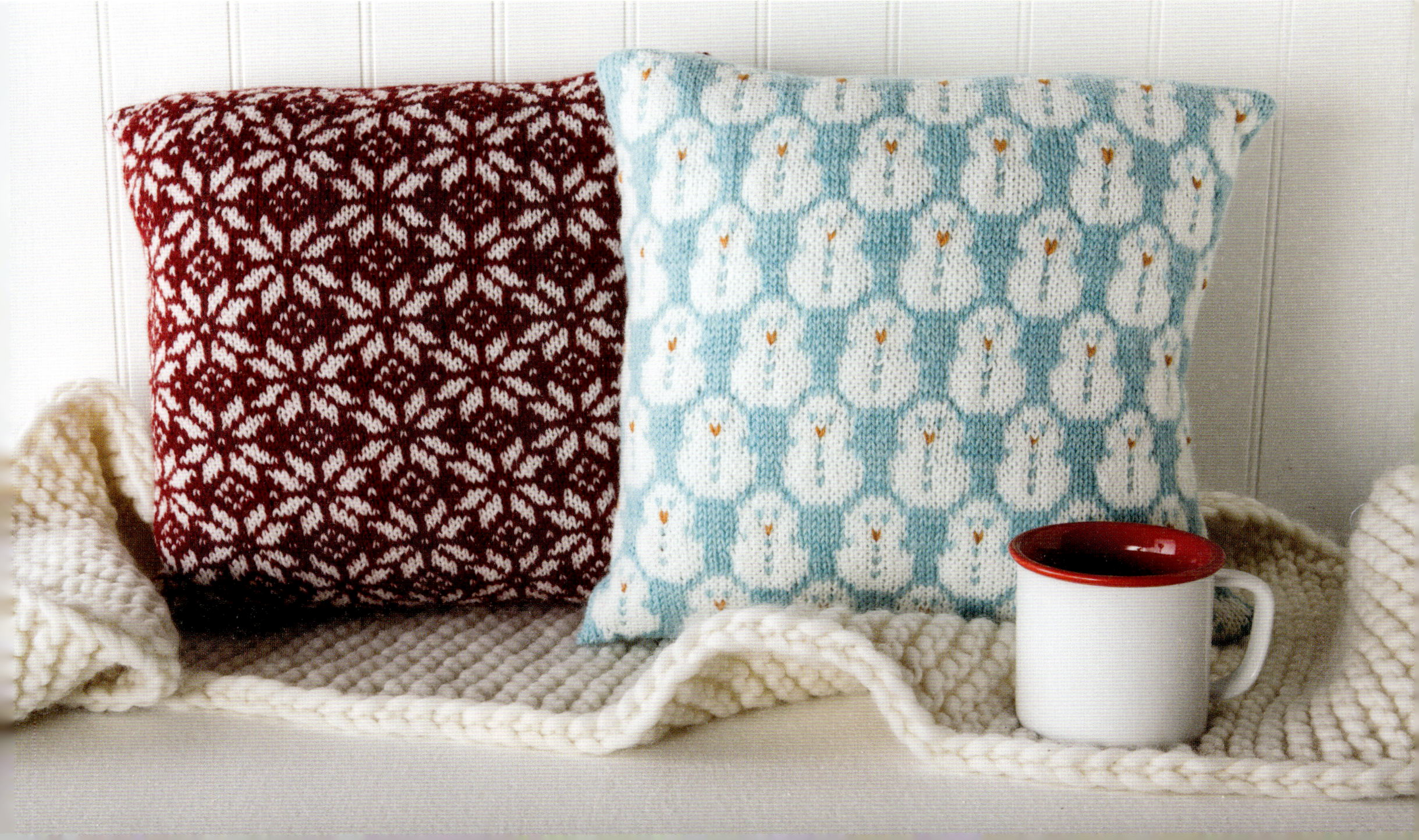

Snowmen Chart A

12	11	10	9	8	7	6	5	4	3	2	1	
■	■	■	■						■	■	■	1

Snowmen Chart B

12	11	10	9	8	7	6	5	4	3	2	1	
		■	■						■	■		24
			■	■	■	■	■	■	■			23
	■			■	■	■	■			■		22
				■	■	■						21
▨			■		■	■						20
			■	■	■	■		■				19
■				■	■	■						18
					■	■						17
■					■	■						16
					■	■						15
■					■	■						14
				■			■					13
			■	■			■	■				12
■	■	■	■						■	■	■	11
■					■		■		■			10
■	■	■							■	■	■	9
■	■	■				▨			■	■	■	8
■	■	■	■						■		■	7
■	■	■				■				■		6
■	■	■									■	5
■	■	■				■					■	4
■	■										■	3
■	■					■					■	2
■	■	■							■	■	■	1

Snowmen Chart C

12	11	10	9	8	7	6	5	4	3	2	1	
■	■	■	■	■				■	■	■	■	1

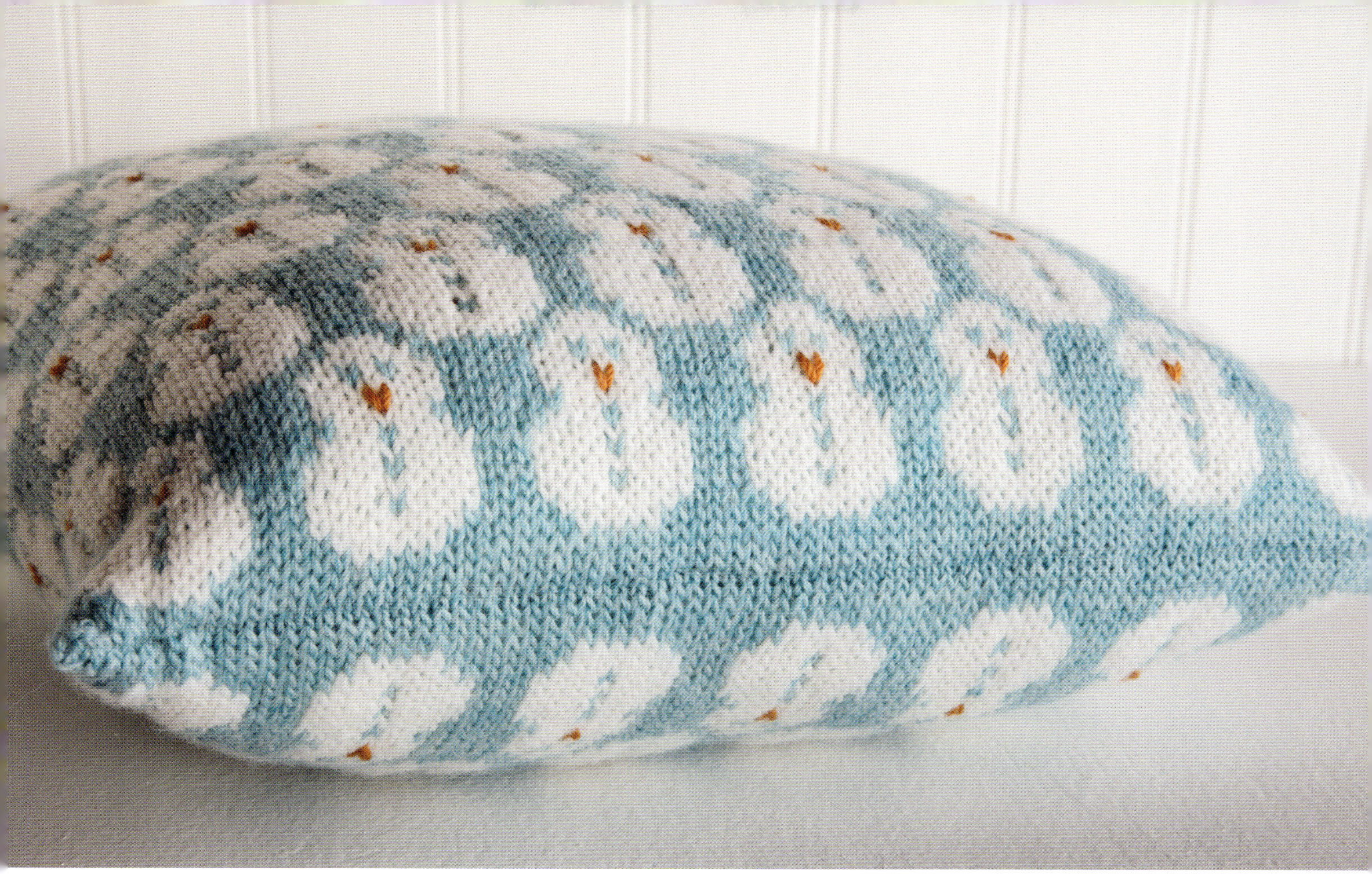

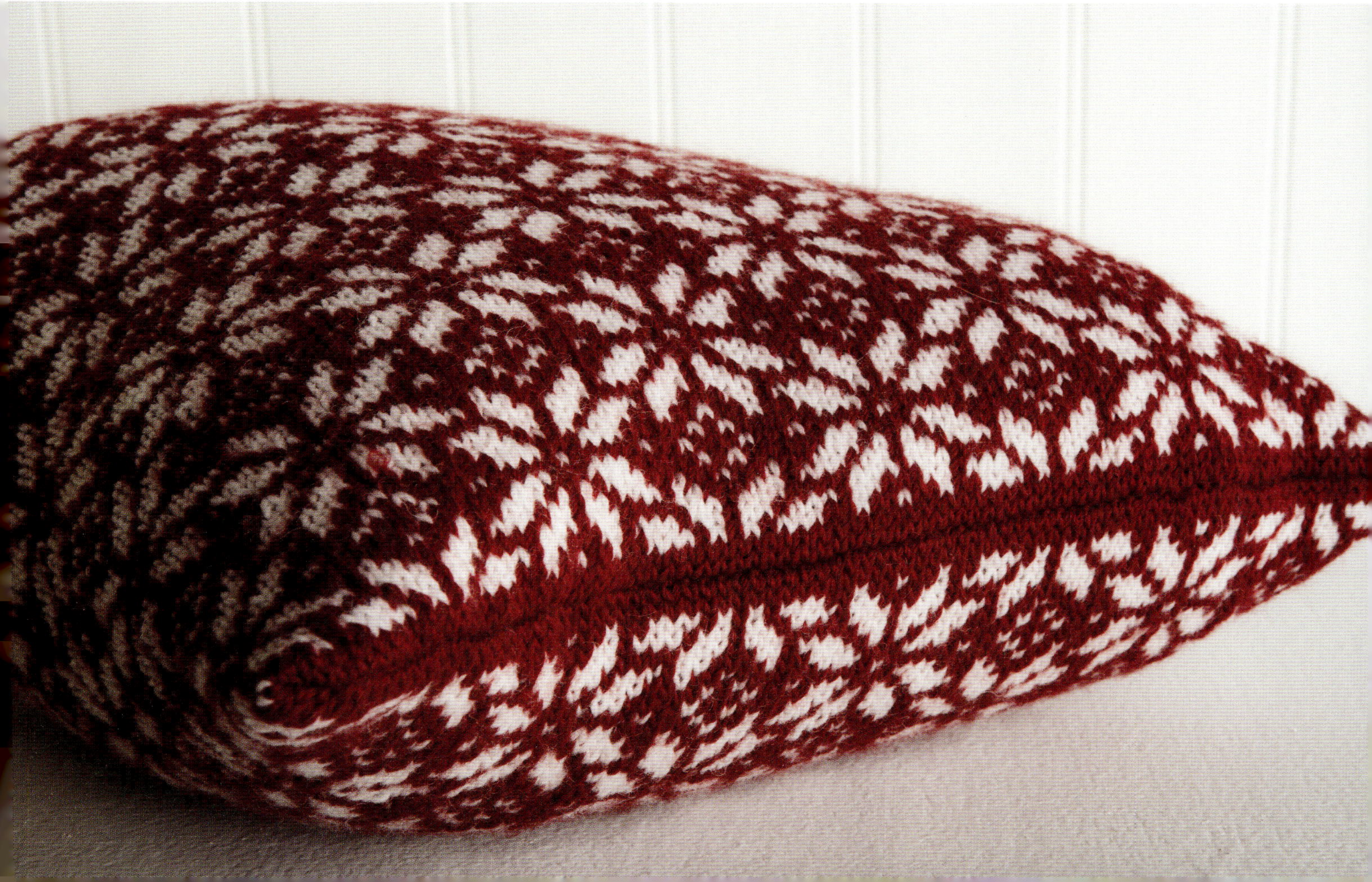

TRIANGLE AND REINDEER STOCKINGS

by Jenny Williams

FINISHED MEASUREMENTS

6.75" wide x 19" long.

YARN

Triangle Stocking:

Knit Picks Wool of the Andes Worsted (100% Peruvian Highland Wool; 110 yards/50g): MC Hollyberry 23419, 2 balls; C1 Cranberry 23425, C2 Fern 23433, C3 Green Tea Heather 24648, C4 Forest Heather 23897, C5 Midnight Heather 25640, C6 Oyster Heather 24649, 1 ball each.

Reindeer Stocking:

Knit Picks Wool of the Andes Worsted (100% Peruvian Highland Wool; 110 yards/50g): MC Hollyberry 23419, 2 balls; C1 Cranberry 23425, C2 Fern 23433, C3 Green Tea Heather 24648, C4 Forest Heather 23897, C5 Midnight Heather 25640, C6 Oyster Heather 24649, 1 ball each.

NEEDLES

US 7 (4.5mm) DPN's or two 24" circular needles for two circulars technique, or one 32" or longer circular needle for Magic Loop technique, or size to obtain gauge.

NOTIONS

Crochet Hook, US 7 (4.5mm) or larger
Yarn Needle
Stitch Markers
Scrap Yarn

GAUGE

23 sts and 25 rows = 4" in stranded St st in the rnd, blocked.

For pattern support, contact
jennyw@tcworks.net

Notes:

These stockings are worked in Stockinette st using the traditional Fair Isle 2-strand method; no more than 2 colors are used on any given row. Worked from the bottom up, it is knit as a straight tube. A provisional cast on and an afterthought heel allow you to work the toe and the heel after the tube is complete. Using duplicate stitch and the charts provided, you can personalize the stocking if you wish.

The charts are worked in the round and knit, read each row from right to left, as a RS row. Both charts are split up into two charts each. Begin with the bottom chart and continue to the top chart.

For a video demonstration of how to work Kitchener st, see
http://tutorials.knitpicks.com/wptutorials/kitchener-stitch/

DIRECTIONS

Both Stockings: Using scrap yarn and the crochet hook, chain 80 sts. Lay the chain face down to view the "purl bumps". Using C6 for Triangle Stocking and MC for Reindeer Stocking, with circular needles PU 78 sts through the purl bumps. PM and join to begin working in the rnd, taking care not to twist sts. K39 sts and PM, to mark beginning of back side, K39 sts.

Triangle Stocking Body

Work Triangle Stocking Chart Row 1, SM, work Triangle Stocking Chart Row 1 again. Cont working Triangle Stocking Chart through Row 31.

Next Rnd, place Scrap Yarn for Afterthought Heel: Work sts 1 – 19 of Triangle Stocking Chart Row 32. Using scrap yarn, K20, SM, K20, Sl these 40 sts back to left needle, continuing with C5, work sts 20 – 39 of Triangle Stocking Chart, SM, work Triangle Stocking Chart Row 32 again. Cont working Triangle Stocking Chart through Row 110.

Reindeer Stocking Body

Work Reindeer Stocking Chart Row 1, SM, work Reindeer Stocking Chart Row 1 again. Cont working Reindeer Stocking Chart through Row 30.

Next Rnd, place Scrap Yarn for Afterthought Heel: Work sts 1 – 19 of Reindeer Stocking Chart Row 31. Using scrap yarn, K20, SM, K20, Sl these 40 sts back to left needle, change to C5, work sts 20 – 39 of Reindeer Stocking Chart, SM, work Reindeer Stocking Chart Row 31 again. Cont working Reindeer Stocking Chart through Row 110.

I-cord Edging

Sl 39 sts. Change to C6 and CO 3 sts onto left needle. (Working yarn will move back and forth between left needle and right needle for the following.) Begin I-cord BO:
Step 1: K2, K2tog TBL.
Step 2: Sl these 3 sts back to left needle.
Rep Steps 1 - 2 to last st.
Next: K2, K2tog, PU 1 st from beginning of I-cord. Sl these 4 sts back to left needle. K2, K2tog. Sl these 3 sts back to left needle, use them for the Hanging Loop, below.

I-cord Hanging Loop

*K3 I-Cord Edging sts. Slide the 3 sts to the right end of the needle and K3. Rep from * for 4". K3tog. BO last st, leaving a tail to sew I-Cord end to Stocking.

Knitting the Afterthought Heel

Remove the scrap yarn which marks the heel and place the 80 live sts on DPN's; 20 sts on bottom front needle, 20 sts on bottom back needle, 20 sts on top front needle, 20 sts on top back needle. Using MC for the Triangle and C4 for the Reindeer, begin at first st on front bottom needle, K40, PM, K40, PM, completing first rnd. 80 sts.

Dec Rnd: K2tog TBL, K to 2 sts before mid rnd M, K2tog, K2tog TBL, K to 2 sts before beginning of rnd M, K2tog. 4 sts dec. Rep Dec Rnd 9 more times, 20 sts remaining between each M.

Place remaining sts on 2 DPNs; back sts between the 2 "hinges" or decrease points on one needle, and front sts between the 2 hinges on the second needle. Graft the heel closed using the Kitchener stitch.

Knitting the Toe

Remove the Provisional CO scrap yarn which marks the toe and place the 78 live sts on 4 DPN's; 19 sts on the first needle, 20 sts on the second, 20 sts on the third needle, and 19 sts on the fourth needle. Join MC for the Triangle and C4 for the Reindeer and K19, PM, K40, PM, K19.

Dec Rnd: K to 2 sts before first M, K2tog, K2tog TBL, K to 2 sts before mid rnd M, K2tog, K2tog TBL, K to end of rnd. 4 sts dec.
Rep Dec Rnd 9 more times, 20 sts remaining between first and second M, 19 sts remaining between second M around to first M.

Place remaining sts on 2 DPNs; back sts between the 2 "hinges" or decrease points on one needle, and front sts between the 2 hinges on the second needle. Graft the toe closed using the Kitchener stitch.

Personalization

Using the Uppercase Letter Chart and the Lowercase Letter Chart, choose the letters with which you wish to personalize the stocking. Thread a yarn needle with C6 and use the duplicate stitch to sew the desired letters to the blank area above the triangles or reindeer on the front of the stocking.

Finishing

Weave in all ends. Sew hanging loop in place. Block using cold water, to prevent colors from running. Gently press out excess water using a towel. For professional looking results, cut a cardboard form to the desired shape and cover it with aluminum foil. Slide damp stocking over the form and allow to dry thoroughly.

Triangle Stocking (Bottom)

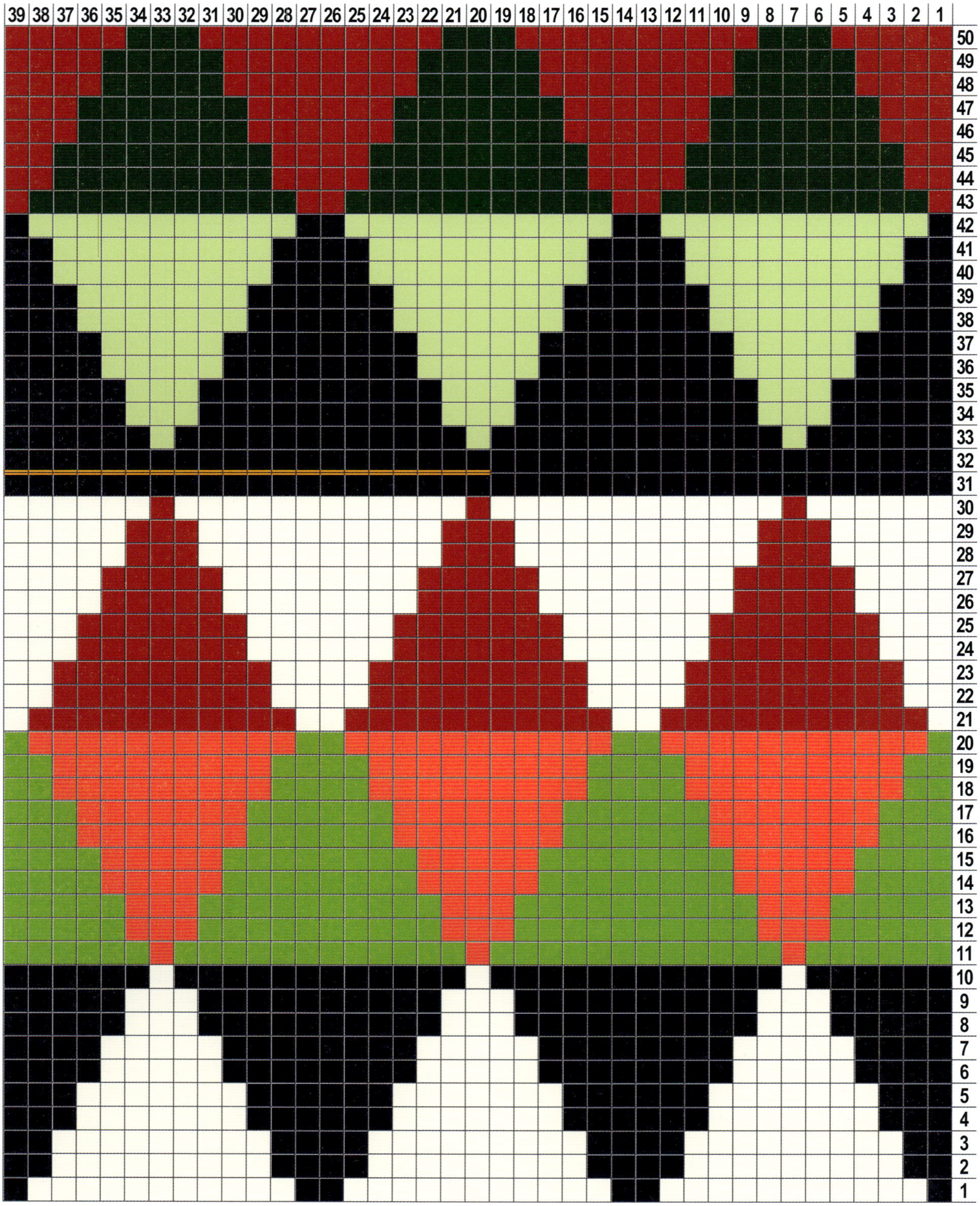

Triangle Stocking (Top)

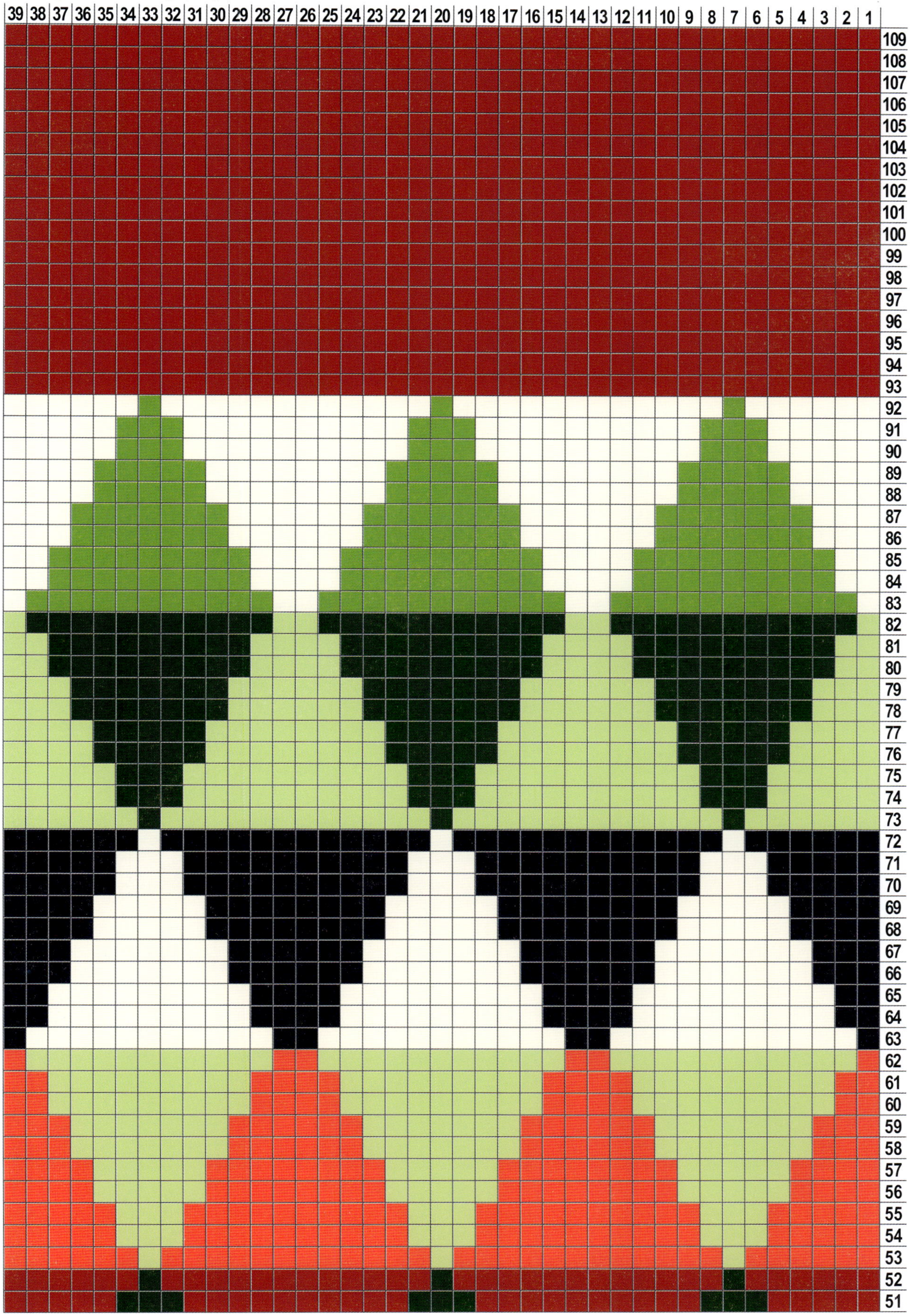

Reindeer Stocking (Top)

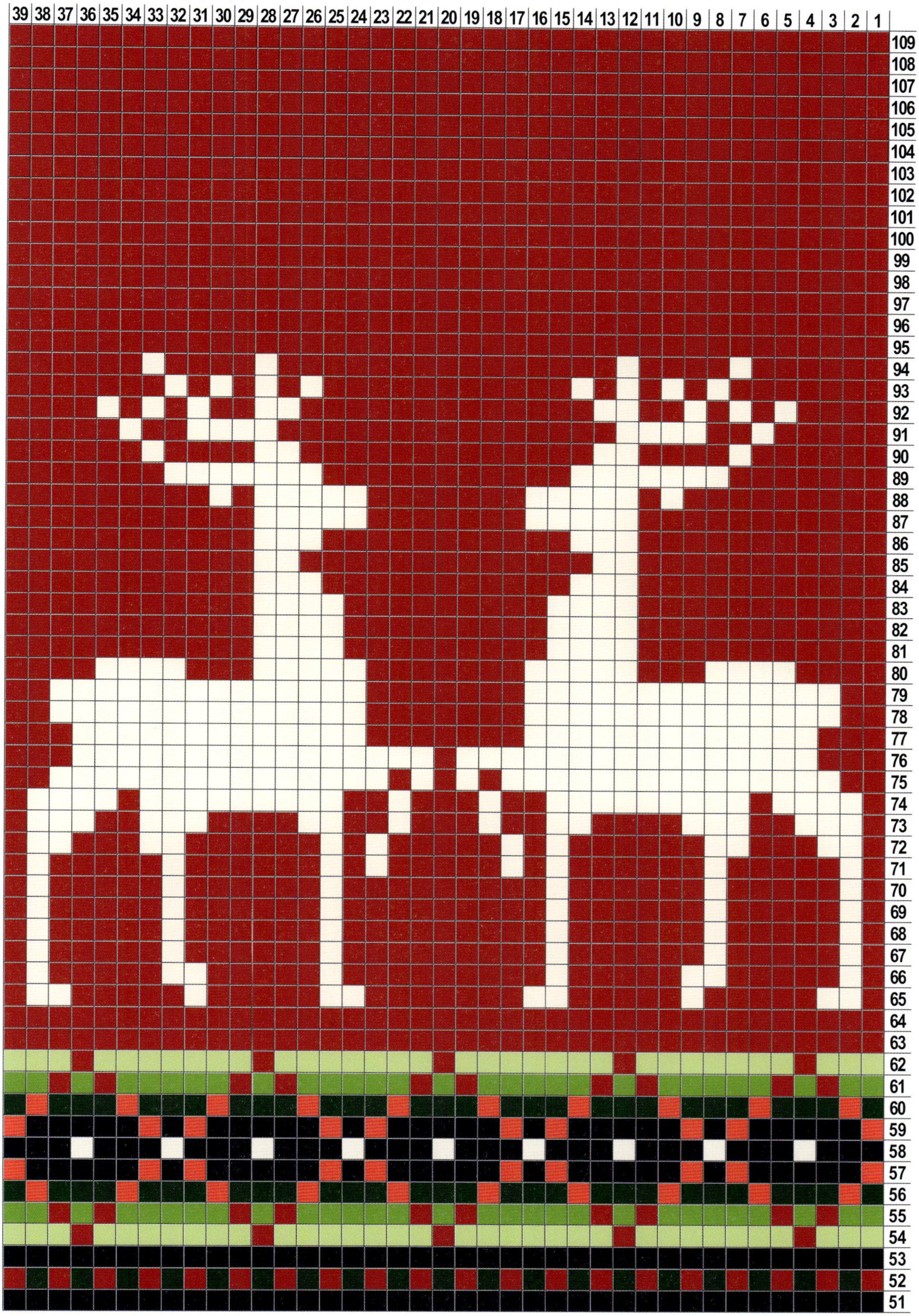

Uppercase Alphabet

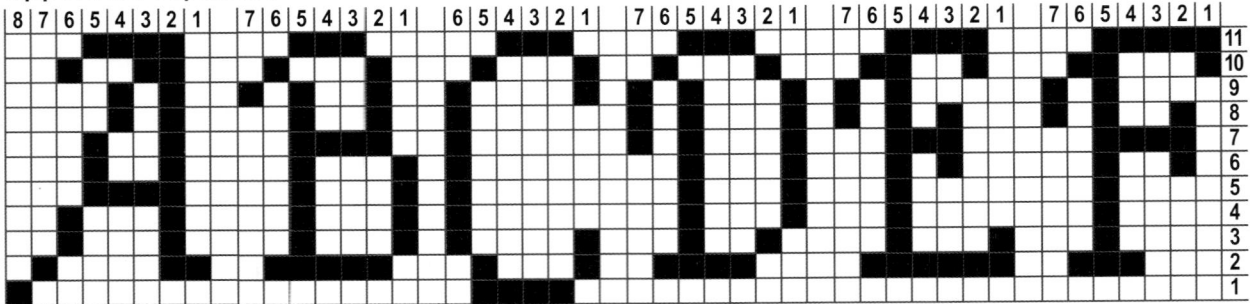

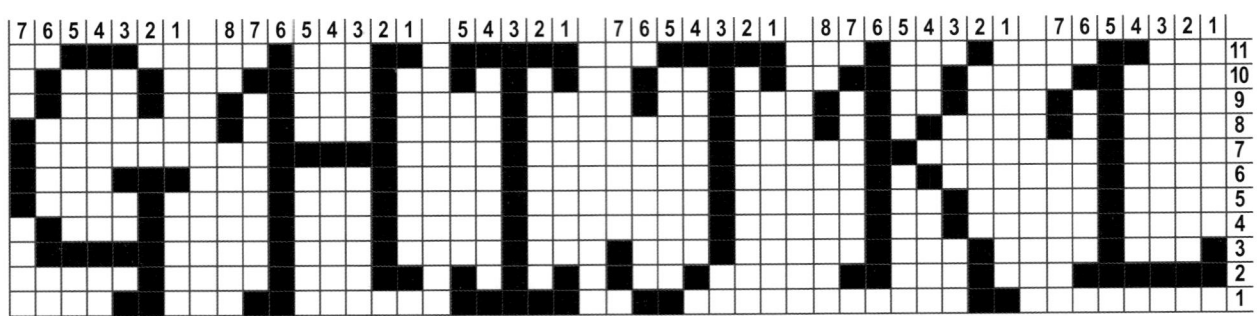

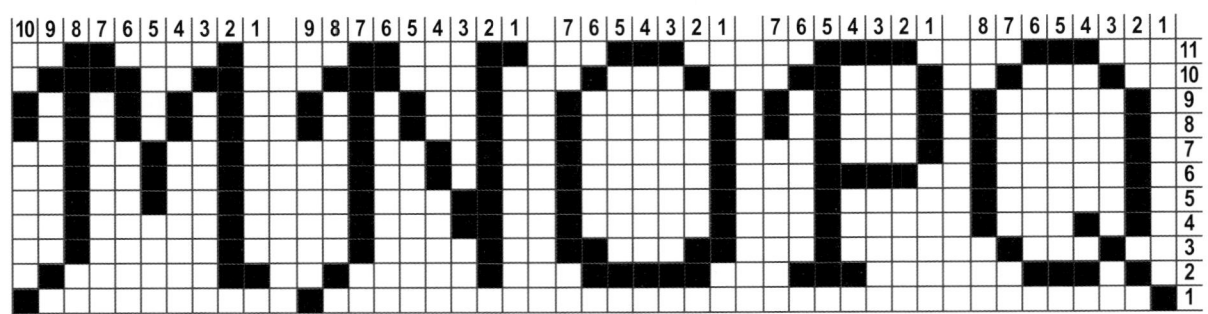

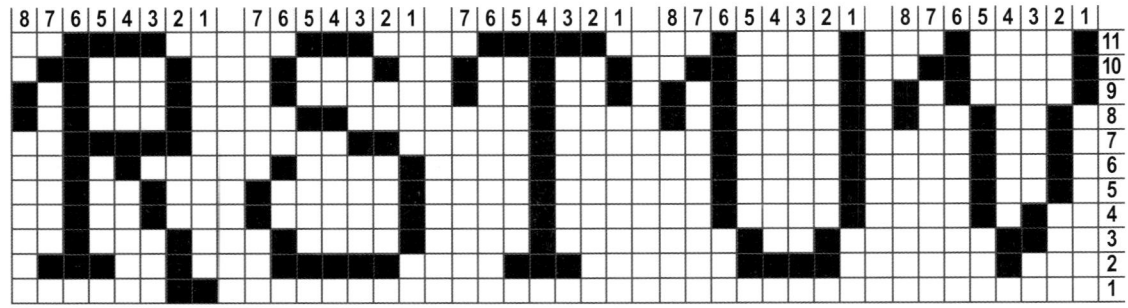

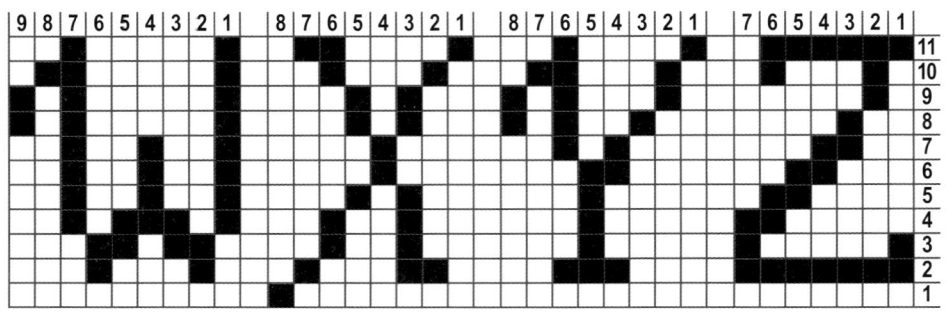

Lowercase Alphabet

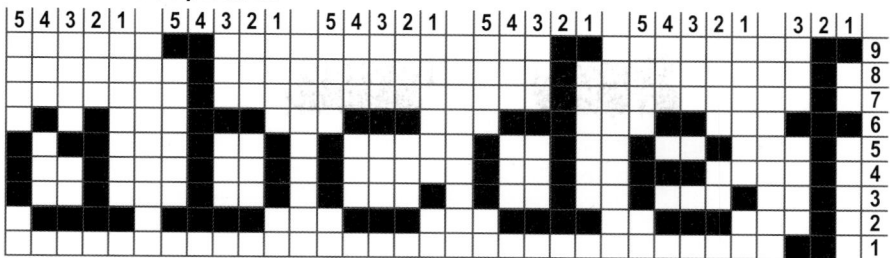

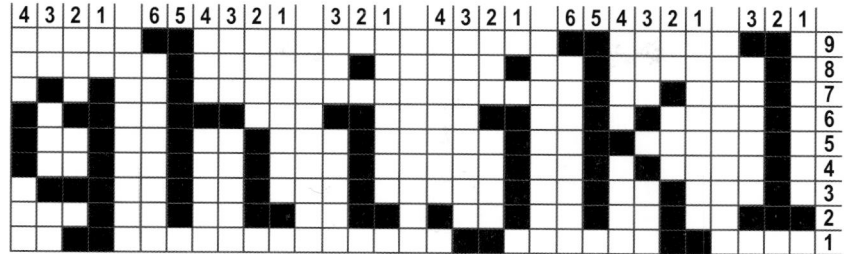

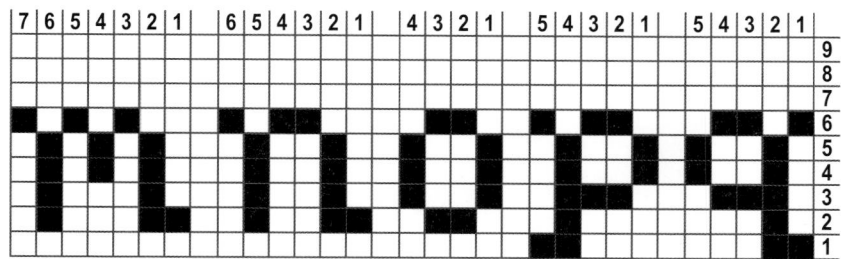

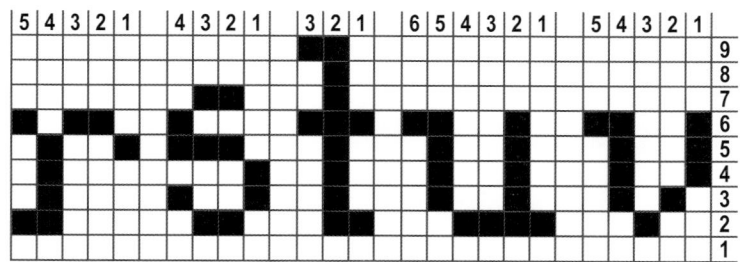

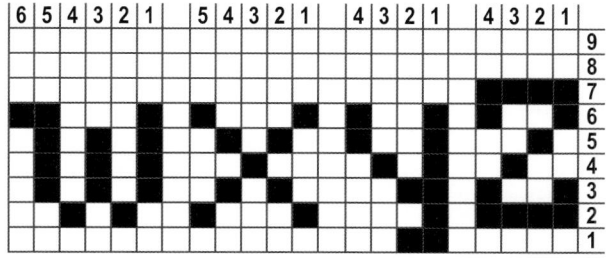

"We make a living by what we get, but we make a life by what we give."

- Winston Churchill

Knit Picks yarn is both luxe and affordable—a seeming contradiction trounced! But it's not just about the pretty colors; we also care deeply about fiber quality and fair labor practices, leaving you with a gorgeously reliable product you'll turn to time and time again.

THIS COLLECTION FEATURES

Wool of the Andes
Worsted & Sport Weights
100% Peruvian Highland Wool

Swish
DK Weight
100% Fine Superwash Merino Wool

Palette
Fingering Weight
100% Peruvian Highland Wool

Wool of the Andes Superwash
Bulky Weight
100% Superwash Wool

Stroll Sock Yarn
Fingering Weight
75% Fine Superwash Merino Wool, 25% Nylon

Glimmer
Fingering Weight
70% Fine Superwash Merino Wool, 25% Nylon, 5% Stellina

View these beautiful yarns and more at www.Knit Picks.com